T0334071

Cambridge Elements ≡

Elements in the Problems of God
edited by
Michael L. Peterson
Asbury Theological Seminary

EVOLUTION AND CHRISTIANITY

Michael Ruse
University of Guelph

CAMBRIDGE
UNIVERSITY PRESS

Shaftesbury Road, Cambridge CB2 8EA, United Kingdom

One Liberty Plaza, 20th Floor, New York, NY 10006, USA

477 Williamstown Road, Port Melbourne, VIC 3207, Australia

314–321, 3rd Floor, Plot 3, Splendor Forum, Jasola District Centre,
New Delhi – 110025, India

103 Penang Road, #05–06/07, Visioncrest Commercial, Singapore 238467

Cambridge University Press is part of Cambridge University Press & Assessment,
a department of the University of Cambridge.

We share the University's mission to contribute to society through the pursuit of
education, learning and research at the highest international levels of excellence.

www.cambridge.org
Information on this title: www.cambridge.org/9781009268967

DOI: 10.1017/9781009268974

First published 2022

A catalogue record for this publication is available from the British Library.

ISBN 978-1-009-26896-7 Paperback
ISSN 2754-8724 (online)
ISSN 2754-8716 (print)

Evolution and Christianity

Elements in the Problems of God

DOI: 10.1017/9781009268974
First published online: December 2022

Michael Ruse
University of Guelph

Author for correspondence: Michael Ruse, mruse@fsu.edu

Abstract: This Element discusses the relationship between Christianity and evolutionary theory, with special emphasis on Darwinian evolutionary theory (Darwinism). The Creationists argue that the two are incompatible and it is religion that is the truth and Darwinism the falsity. The New Atheists argue that the two are incompatible and it is religion that is the falsity and Darwinism the truth. Through a careful examination of both Darwinian theory and Christianity, this Element shows that both extremes are mistaken. It accepts that there are difficult issues to be solved, for example the problem of evil – which some think is exacerbated by Darwinism – and the necessary appearance of *Homo sapiens* – which is problematic if evolutionary theory does not guarantee progress and the evolution of humans as the apotheosis. However, it argues that there are ways forward and that Christianity and evolutionary thinking can be shown to be compatible.

Keywords: Christianity, Darwinism, warfare, independence, integration

ISBNs: 9781009268967 (PB), 9781009268974 (OC)
ISSNs: 2754-8724 (online), 2754-8716 (print)

Contents

Prologue

In 1859, the English naturalist Charles Robert Darwin published his epoch-making work *On the Origin of Species by Means of Natural Selection, or the Preservation of Favoured Races in the Struggle for Life* (Darwin 1859). At once, his old friend and mentor Adam Sedgwick, ordained Anglican minister and Professor of Geology at Cambridge University, wrote:

> If I did not think you a good tempered & truth loving man I should not tell you that, (spite of the great knowledge; store of facts; capital views of the corelations of the various parts of organic nature; admirable hints about the diffusions, thro' wide regions, of nearly related organic beings; &c &c) I have read your book with more pain than pleasure. Parts of it I admired greatly; parts I laughed at till my sides were almost sore; other parts I read with absolute sorrow; because I think them utterly false & grievously mischievous.
> (Letter from Sedgwick to Darwin, 24 November 1859, Darwin Correspondence Project – DCP-LETT-2548))

The next year, 1860, at the annual meeting of the British Association for the Advancement of Science, at Oxford, Bishop Samuel Wilberforce, high Anglican Bishop of Oxford (and son of William Wilberforce of slave-trade-abolition fame), squared off against Darwin's bulldog Thomas Henry Huxley, a professor at the Royal School of Mines. Supposedly, the bishop asked the professor if he was descended from monkeys on his grandmother's side or his grandfather's side; the professor replied that he had sooner be descended from a monkey than from a bishop of the Church of England. All rather exaggerated and one of those good tales where there is more truth in fiction than in fact (Lucas 1979).

Across the Atlantic, Swiss-born Harvard professor Louis Agassiz, Unitarian, wrote to Charles Darwin: 'It is true that I am and have been from the beginning an uncompromising opponent of your views concerning the transmutability of species, it is equally true that I hold these views as mischievous, because they lead to a looseness of argumentation which it has been the aim of the great naturalists of our age to eliminate' (Agassiz 1885, letter of 22 July 1868). In the same vein, Charles Hodge, the principal of the Princeton Theological Seminary, wrote a book published in 1874 with the title *What Is Darwinism?* At the end of the book, he answered his own question: 'What is Darwinism? It is atheism' (Hodge 1874, 177). This was a tradition that flourished. It is little wonder that, as the century went by, books were being published with titles like *History of the Conflict Between Religion and Science* (Draper 1875) and *History of the Warfare of Science with Theology in Christendom* (White 1896).

The pattern was set. On the one side, the religious – especially those with literalist yearnings. The 'Creation Scientists' wrote books – Duane T.

Gish's (1973) *Evolution: The Fossils Say No!* was an immediate bestseller – debated evolutionists – usually with much success because they were adept at making your average scientist lose his temper and look silly – and went after their opponents. Henry M. Morris – co-author of the seminal *Genesis Flood* (Whitcomb and Morris 1961) – in a review of one of my books, in a tone more pitying than critical, concludes: 'One thing he does not do, however, in any of his books, is to prove macroevolution, or even to show it to be as probable as creation' (Morris 1999, n.p.). On the other side were the scientists – today, especially those part of or sympathetic to the so-called New Atheists. In *The God Delusion*, Richard Dawkins says, 'Faith is an evil precisely because it requires no justification' (Dawkins 2006, 308). Jerry Coyne, an eminent (and enthusiastic) Darwinian evolutionist, spoke for many when he described the *Origin* as the 'greatest scripture killer ever penned', continuing that 'science and religion are engaged in a kind of war: a war for understanding, a war about whether we should have good reasons for what we accept as true' (Coyne 2015, 20).

Expectedly, not everyone feels or has felt this way. Charles Darwin strongly eschewed claims about warfare and incompatibility. Obviously, he saw that his thinking was going to impinge on some views that religious people do or have taken seriously, and he was not beyond thinking that there can be tensions. However, his major difficulties with religion were theological, not scientific. He hated the idea that people might be condemned for their honest beliefs. 'I can indeed hardly see how anyone ought to wish Christianity to be true; for if so the plain language of the text seems to show that the men who do not believe, and this would include my Father, Brother and almost all my best friends, will be everlastingly punished. And this is a damnable doctrine' (Darwin 1958, 87). Generally, Darwin thought that science and religion can and should go their various ways. His closest personal friend was Brodie Innes, the local Anglican vicar. Late in life, after retirement, the man of God wrote to his friend, the man of science: 'I must say I am indebted to you for much confirmation of the view ... that Science and Religion should go on separately, and not contest in any way' (letter from Innes to Darwin, 1 December 1878, DCP-LETT-11768). Darwin made it very clear that he was simply not interested in attempts to reconcile science and religion. To a correspondent who was trying to arrange a conference demonstrating the compatibility of science and religion, he wrote: 'I can see no prospect of any benefit arising from the proposed conference' (letter to W. R. Brown, 18 December 1880).

It is these, and other, different perspectives on the science–religion relationship, specifically the evolution–Christianity relationship, that I want to consider in this Element. The structure of what follows is straightforward. We begin with a brief history of evolutionary thinking, looking at its beginnings, at the contribution of Charles Darwin and then of later developments – scientific and cultural – of his ideas. We shall see that two root metaphors, the world-as-organism and the world-as-machine, have a crucial role to play in this account. We move next to the basic claims of Christianity. In this section, as in the first, the discussion is intentionally entirely non-judgemental. Third, we shall look at the interactions, actual and possible, between the claims of Sections 1 and 2.

To conclude, in a brief Epilogue, I shall refer to a well-known, fourfold division of possible science–religion relationships proposed by the physicist-theologian Ian Barbour (1990): (1) *conflict*, where both sides 'claim that science and theology make rival literal statements about the same domain, the history of nature, so that one must choose between them' (Barbour 1990, 4); (2) *independence*, where '[p]roponents of this view say there are two jurisdictions and each party must keep off the other's turf. Each must tend to its own business and not meddle in the affairs of the other' (Barbour 1990, 10); (3) *dialogue*, where '[t]he aim should be 'consonance but not direct implication', which implies that in the end the two sets of assertions are not, after all, totally independent' (Barbour 1990, 16); and (4) *integration*, where this 'final group of authors holds that some sort of integration is possible between the content of theology and the content of science' (Barbour 1990, 23). These divisions are not to be taken as gospel, as one might say; they are also not to be taken as Newtonian, as one might equally say. But they will help to put things in perspective.

As we set out, I want to reveal – stress – what I believe is the key to understanding the relationship between Christianity and evolution, Darwinian evolution in particular. The latter is the offspring of the former – some would say the illegitimate offspring of the former. Darwin's theory of evolution could not have existed without the Christian religion. Idea after idea, concept after concept, puzzle after puzzle starts with Christianity; Darwin's theory takes them up, incorporates them and tries to give its own secular explanation. In suggesting the word 'illegitimate', I do not intend negative connotations. Rather, I point to the undoubted fact that the emergence of Darwinian thinking was not the intent of Christian thinkers or always entirely welcomed by them. This, however, is the truth and we must understand the implications.

1 Evolution

Root Metaphors

The start of the Scientific Revolution, that major change in worldviews that occurred in the sixteenth and seventeenth centuries, is usually dated from 1543, when the Polish cleric and astronomer Nicolaus Copernicus published *De revolutionibus orbium coelestium – On the Revolutions of the Heavenly Spheres –* in which he argued that the Earth goes around the sun (celestial motion) rather than the sun around the Earth (terrestrial motion). The end is usually dated from 1687, when the English physicist Isaac Newton published *Philosophiæ Naturalis Principia Mathematica – Mathematical Principles of Natural Philosophy* – in which he showed that his theory of gravitational attraction could explain the main claims of the Revolution, in particular the celestial laws of planetary motion of Johannes Kepler and the terrestrial laws of bodies in motion of Galileo Galilei. This all said, the general opinion of historians of those great events is that the real change is one of what linguists call 'root metaphors', basic conceptual frameworks akin to Thomas Kuhn's (1962) 'paradigms', from the world seen as an organism – *organicism* – to the world seen as a machine – *mechanism* (Hall 1983; Dijksterhuis 1961).

Plato in the *Timaeus* set the scene for the organic model or metaphor. Explicitly he argued that the Creator, the Demiurge, also the Form of the Good, moulded the universe on the lines of an organism: 'he put intelligence in soul and soul in body, and framed the universe to be the best and fairest work in the order of nature, and the world became a living soul through the providence of God' (*Timaeus*, in Cooper 1997, 30b–c). Aristotle did not, could not, see the world as an organism created or designed by God. Apart from anything else, his Unmoved Mover spends all eternity contemplating its own perfection – remind you of some teenagers you know? – knowing nothing of the physical world (Sedley 2008). But Aristotle was no less an organicist than Plato, seeing all things striving to the Mover, to perfection. Well known is his discussion of causation, distinguishing 'efficient causes' – the hammer striking the nail and making the sound – from 'final causes' – the nail being driven in in order to build the house. We are going from causes about the past and present to causes about the future. Today, this way of conceptualizing things is generally called 'teleological'. This kind of thinking was embraced by the great Christian philosophers/theologians, notably Augustine and Aquinas.

By the end of the Middle Ages, with the rise of machines – particularly clocks and pumps – the metaphor was running out of steam, to use an appropriate image. People started to think in terms of systems working according to eternal, unbroken laws. To quote the great chemist Robert Boyle:

> [The world] is like a rare clock, such as may be that at Strasbourg, where all things are so skillfully contrived that the engine being once set a-moving, all things proceed according to the artificer's first design, and the motions of the little statues that at such hours perform these or those motions do not require (like those of puppets) the peculiar interposing of the artificer or any intelligent agent employed by him, but perform their functions on particular occasions by virtue of the general and primitive contrivance of the whole engine.
>
> (Boyle [1686] 1996, 12–13)

While there might be design, final cause, within the system – the valve is there in order to control the escape of the steam – overall there is no meaning or purpose. In the words of the English philosopher Francis Bacon, final causes are akin to Vestal Virgins – beautiful but sterile.

Evolution

With the change in root metaphors came a change in theological perspectives. Hitherto, God had been hovering over His creation, and all value came directly from him. *Providence!*. Away from the Creator, nothing we can do has any meaning.

> When I survey the wondrous cross
> on which the Prince of glory died,
> my richest gain I count but loss,
> and pour contempt on all my pride.
> (from the hymn 'When I Survey the Wondrous
> Cross', Isaac Watts 1707)

Now the emphasis changed to us doing things for ourselves. The laws of nature are there. They make things work. Now get on with it. From providence, we arrived at *progress*. And with this came evolutionary speculations, the thought that organisms might not have been created in one fell swoop by a hands-on Creator but have come naturally through the working of unbroken law. From a providential view of origins to a progressivist view.

In one sense, the move to evolution was no great surprise. From the time of Aristotle, people had accepted the idea of a 'chain of being', that organisms could be assigned to a level on an upwards scale or ladder (Lovejoy 1936; see also Figure 1). Although static, it fitted in nicely with the organicist vision, from lowly acorn to mighty oak. We had a rise from the lowliest forms to the highest, human beings, and if one was so inclined one could keep going through the orders of angels until one reached God. Now with the idea of progress, with laws moving everything, rather than intervening Providence, we have an escalator rather than a staircase. In the middle of the eighteenth century, we find the French man of letters Denis Diderot, who combined a happy career of writing pornographic novels about lesbian nuns with floating speculations about natural origins (Ruse 2005). More staid, but as committed to such ideas, was Charles Darwin's grandfather, Erasmus Darwin, who hymned evolution in prose and verse.

> Organic Life beneath the shoreless waves
> Was born and nurs'd in Ocean's pearly caves;
> First forms minute, unseen by spheric glass,
> Move on the mud, or pierce the watery mass;

Figure 1 The great chain of being – God, angels, heaven, humans, beasts, plants, flame, rocks – from Ramon Lull's *Ladder of Ascent and Descent of the Mind*, 1305

These, as successive generations bloom,
New powers acquire, and larger limbs assume;
Whence countless groups of vegetation spring,
And breathing realms of fin, and feet, and wing.
Thus the tall Oak, the giant of the wood,
Which bears Britannia's thunders on the flood;
The Whale, unmeasured monster of the main,

> The lordly Lion, monarch of the plain,
> The Eagle soaring in the realms of air,
> Whose eye undazzled drinks the solar glare,
> Imperious man, who rules the bestial crowd,
> Of language, reason, and reflection proud,
> With brow erect who scorns this earthy sod,
> And styles himself the image of his God;
> Arose from rudiments of form and sense,
> An embryo point, or microscopic ens!
> (Darwin 1803, vol. 1, 11, ll. 295–314)

Explicitly, Erasmus Darwin tied his evolutionary biology in with his progressivist philosophy of life. The idea of organic progressive evolution 'is analogous to the improving excellence observable in every part of the creation; such as the progressive increase of the wisdom and happiness of its inhabitants' (Darwin [1794–6] 1801, vol. 2, 247).

In the age of Newton, some thought had to be given to causes. Erasmus Darwin more or less assumed an internal motion upwards, as with organic growth – acorn to oak – but he added a secondary mechanism, one that goes back to the Old Testament, the inheritance of acquired characteristics. A decade or so later, this secondary mechanism was adopted by the French systematist Jean Baptiste de Lamarck, the most famous of all the pre-Charles Darwin evolutionists. Indeed, it goes by his name, 'Lamarckism'; although, as with Erasmus Darwin, it is a secondary mechanism to the internal forces pushing organisms ever up the scale (Burkhardt 1977). Not that either was received with unalloyed approval. Lamarck was opposed in France by the most famous biologist of his age, Georges Cuvier, and in England by just about every leading scientist. In 1844, anonymously, the Scottish publisher Robert Chambers had produced an evolutionary tract, *Vestiges of the Natural History of Creation* (Chambers 1844). Fire descended upon him, from Adam Sedgwick in Cambridge, from David Brewster, a physicist from Scotland, and from William Whewell, a scientist (he worked on the tides), historian and philosopher of science, and a powerful university administrator; he was master of Trinity College, Cambridge (Secord 2000). To be candid, Chambers did not have a great deal of new information, but he did make strongly the point about progress.

> A progression resembling development may be traced in human nature, both in the individual and in large groups of men .... Now all of this is in conformity with what we have seen of the progress of organic creation. It seems but the minute hand of a watch, of which the hour hand is the transition from species to species. Knowing what we do of that latter transition, the possibility of a decided and general retrogression of the highest species towards a meaner type is scarce admissible, but a forward movement seems anything but unlikely. (Chambers 1846, 401–2)

Charles Darwin

It was to be another fifteen years before the *Origin* was published, but already privately it was well on the way (Browne 1995). Charles Darwin (1809–82) came from a rich, upper-middle-class family. His maternal grandfather was Josiah Wedgwood, the potter, and one of the most successful businessmen of his day. More family money came from this source when he married his first cousin, Emma Wedgwood. Educated first at an English private ('public') school, followed by an abortive attempt to study medicine at Edinburgh, Darwin ended up at the University of Cambridge, intending to become an Anglican clergyman, a respectable position for a rather aimless man with a good private income. However, his talents as a biologist were spotted by mentoring faculty (including the Professor of Botany, John Henslow, as well as Sedgwick and Whewell) and in 1831 he got the offer to go as ship's naturalist on HMS *Beagle*. He was to spend five years mostly mapping the coast of South America – a major market for British industrially produced goods – ending by going all the way around the globe before returning to England. Darwin did not become an evolutionist on the trip; but when, on his return, a leading taxonomist assured him that the different kinds of birds he had captured on the Galapagos Archipelago in the Pacific were indeed different species, he crossed the divide. It made no sense that independently created, but similar species had by coincidence found their ways to adjoining islands. Especially since they were all so similar to birds on the nearest mainland (and not at all to Africa). It had to be (what Darwin was to call) 'descent with modification' and – as a private notebook entry shows – it implies that all of nature is connected on a tree of life (see Figure 2).

It was still the age of Newton – Whewell was fanatical – and so causes had to be sought. The chief one, natural selection, was discovered at the end of September 1838. (Darwin kept detailed notebooks so we can follow his enquiries and speculations.) Britain's Industrial Revolution had started in the eighteenth century. Such a revolution demands a parallel agricultural revolution. People are leaving the land to move to factories in cities – fewer to produce the food – and, once the move has been made, there is a priority on large families because children can do work on machines that is impossible for adults – more mouths to feed. Hence, there must be improved ways of producing food and selective breeding, animals and plants, is an obvious and powerful option. Darwin came from Shropshire, the heart of rural England, so he knew much about breeding, especially given that his uncle Josh (son of the first Josiah Wedgwood and father of Emma) was a gentleman farmer. Unsurprisingly, Darwin – who read quickly and widely – seized on selection as a possible

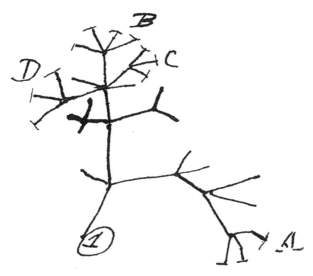

Figure 2 Darwin's first sketch of the tree of life, from a notebook early in 1837

cause, especially since some of his sources themselves drew an analogy between selection in nature and selection by breeders.

> A severe winter, or a scarcity of food, by destroying the weak or unhealthy, has all the good effects of the most skilful selection. In cold and barren countries no animal can live to the age of maturity, but those who have strong constitutions; the weak and the unhealthy do not live to propagate their infirmities, as is too often the case with our domestic animals. To this I attribute the peculiar hardiness of the horses, cattle, and sheep, bred in mountainous countries, more than their having been inured to the severity of climate. (Sebright 1809, 15–16)

But how to get this to work universally and efficiently? In September 1838, at the recommendation of his older brother (also called) Erasmus, Charles Darwin read a book by yet another Anglican clergyman, the Reverend Thomas Robert Malthus: *An Essay on a Principle of Population* (Malthus [1826] 1914). Malthus (as had many) took note of the rapidly increasing population. He argued that God controls it through a 'struggle for existence'. More organisms are born than can survive and reproduce. Hence there will be a kind of culling and population numbers eventually are kept in check. Darwin seized on this as the motive force, the pressure, behind a general process of selection – he did not use the term 'natural selection' until a year or two later – and, given enough time, evolution would occur. Darwin never rejected Lamarckism, but now he had his main cause of change, a kind of biological equivalent to the Newtonian force of gravitational attraction.

Darwin – who lived on family riches and who at this time was publicly primarily writing up the results of the *Beagle* trip, as well as what was to become a very popular travel-book account of his time in South America and the rest of the voyage – in 1842 wrote a short *Sketch* of his views and, in 1844, a much-extended *Essay* (Darwin 1909). He did not publish. Not because, as is sometimes suggested, he himself worried about what he had to say. That was never an issue. He had fallen very sick with what was to be an ongoing-but-unknown debilitating illness – nausea, loss of appetite, diarrhoea and more. Today, the suggestion is that he might have been suffering from lactose intolerance. Yet, the main reason for the delay was undoubtedly the harsh reaction of his fellow scientists – many his teachers and mentors – to the evolutionary speculations of Chambers. Darwin knew he had a real theory – but still. So, he sat on his ideas until the arrival of an essay in 1858 by a junior naturalist, Alfred Russel Wallace (1858), with virtually the same ideas (arrived at independently) pushed him into action. Quickly he wrote up an extended book, and the *Origin of Species* arrived in the autumn of 1859.

The *Origin*

The *Origin* is written in a user-friendly style – no mathematics for a start! – but looks deceive. It is a very carefully structured work (see Figure 3). It is intended to be Newtonian – after all, Darwin, like Newton, was a Cambridge graduate – and, to this end, Darwin wanted to show the status and importance of natural selection. It was to be not just a cause but a *vera causa*, a true cause (Ruse 1975). This was how Newton described the force of gravitational attraction, starting generations of discussion about what exactly that meant. The physicist-philosopher John F. W. Herschel, in his *Preliminary Discourse on the Study of Natural Philosophy* (Herschel 1830), took what might be called an empiricist approach to the matter. That a true cause is embedded in an axiomatic system – premises or hypotheses at the top, empirical laws to be inferred – was taken as granted, with Newton's law of gravitational attraction as a premise and Kepler's and Galileo's laws as consequences. What of the force itself? Herschel said that we knew it existed and did what was claimed – was a *vera causa* – because we can pinpoint it by analogy. If a cause is like something of which we have personal knowledge or acquaintance, then its existence and power are that much more reasonable. The reason we think that there is a force pulling the moon to the Earth as it circles it is that we have had the experience of a stone whirling at the end of a piece of string and know that a force is needed to keep it in place. Under its own power it would shoot off into space.

Whewell (1840) took a rationalist approach to the *vera causa* problem. The reason we look at a cause as real is that hypotheses incorporating it can explain

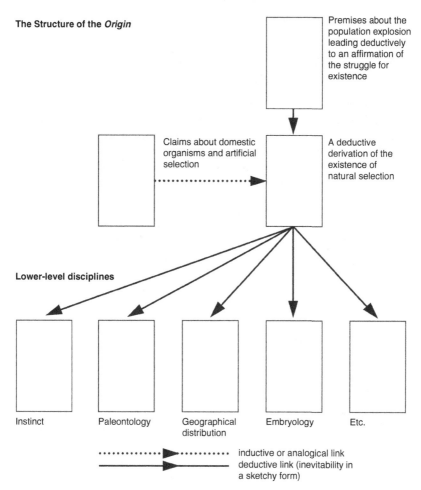

The Structure of the *Origin*

Premises about the population explosion leading deductively to an affirmation of the struggle for existence

Claims about domestic organisms and artificial selection

A deductive derivation of the existence of natural selection

Lower-level disciplines

Instinct

Paleontology

Geographical distribution

Embryology

Etc.

inductive or analogical link

deductive link (inevitability in a sketchy form)

Figure 3 The structure of the argument in the *Origin*, showing the three parts

many disparate things. In the case of Newtonian force, it can explain both that which occurs in the heavens – Kepler – and that which occurs down here on Earth – Galileo. It breaks down the hitherto sacrosanct division between the pure unchanging heavens and the messy world in which we live. You don't have to experience the force, just the consequences. By example, Whewell brought up the wave theory (undulatory theory) of light. For 150 years, people thought that Newton was right – light is a mélange of little corpuscles. Then, at the beginning of the nineteenth century, a number of experiments swung people to Huygens' hypothesis that light is waves. The important point is that opinion was not swung by direct acquaintance with waves. It was the consequences that counted.

Clever Charles Darwin covered his options. First, he showed that natural selection is reasonable by virtue of the success of artificial selection. It is something of which people have hands-on experience. The Herschel-type empiricist *vera causa*. Then he argued (in an admittedly rather informal way) that the cause is embedded in an axiom system. We have the overall Newtonian pattern in which the *vera causa* is embedded. First, to the struggle for existence:

> A struggle for existence inevitably follows from the high rate at which all organic beings tend to increase. Every being, which during its natural lifetime produces several eggs or seeds, must suffer destruction during some period of its life, and during some season or occasional year, otherwise, on the principle of geometrical increase, its numbers would quickly become so inordinately great that no country could support the product. Hence, as more individuals are produced than can possibly survive, there must in every case be a struggle for existence, either one individual with another of the same species, or with the individuals of distinct species, or with the physical conditions of life. It is the doctrine of Malthus applied with manifold force to the whole animal and vegetable kingdoms; for in this case there can be no artificial increase of food, and no prudential restraint from marriage. Although some species may be now increasing, more or less rapidly, in numbers, all cannot do so, for the world would not hold them. (Darwin 1859, 63–4)

Then to natural selection:

> HOW will the struggle for existence, discussed too briefly in the last chapter, act in regard to variation? Can the principle of selection, which we have seen is so potent in the hands of man, apply in nature? I think we shall see that it can act most effectually. Let it be borne in mind in what an endless number of strange peculiarities our domestic productions, and, in a lesser degree, those under nature, vary; and how strong the hereditary tendency is. Under domestication, it may be truly said that the whole organisation becomes in some degree plastic. Let it be borne in mind how infinitely complex and close-fitting are the mutual relations of all organic beings to each other and to their physical conditions of life. Can it, then, be thought improbable, seeing that variations useful to man have undoubtedly occurred, that other variations useful in some way to each being in the great and complex battle of life, should sometimes occur in the course of thousands of generations? If such do occur, can we doubt (remembering that many more individuals are born than can possibly survive) that individuals having any advantage, however slight, over others, would have the best chance of surviving and of procreating their kind? On the other hand, we may feel sure that any variation in the least degree injurious would be rigidly destroyed. This preservation of favourable variations and the rejection of injurious variations, I call Natural Selection. (Darwin 1859, 80–1)

After this, Darwin added some extra insights. There was a secondary mechanism, sexual selection – struggle within the species for mates – then the reasons for speciation. A function of the division of labour: 'in the general economy of any land, the more widely and perfectly the animals and plants are diversified for different habits of life, so will a greater number of individuals be capable of there supporting themselves' (116). And then, summing up, the tree of life. The big picture:

> As buds give rise by growth to fresh buds, and these, if vigorous, branch out and overtop on all sides many a feebler branch, so by generation I believe it has been with the great Tree of Life, which fills with its dead and broken branches the crust of the earth, and covers the surface with its ever branching and beautiful ramifications. (Darwin 1859, 129–30)

And now, third, the Whewellian rationalist *vera causa*. Whewell (1840) spoke of the different branches of empirical enquiry coming together under a uniting hypothesis as a 'consilience of inductions'. Darwin offered a paradigm case. He ran through the organic world showing how all comes together under natural selection. First social behaviour, showing how sterile workers can be selected, so long as close relatives breed. Today this is known as kin selection.

> As ants work by inherited instincts and by inherited tools or weapons, and not by acquired knowledge and manufactured instruments, a perfect division of labour could be effected with them only by the workers being sterile; for had they been fertile, they would have intercrossed, and their instincts and structure would have become blended. And nature has, as I believe, effected this admirable division of labour in the communities of ants, by the means of natural selection. (Darwin 1859, 241–2)

Then palaeontology and the fossil record. Many puzzling facts are explained. For instance, it seems that certain basic forms evolve apart under natural selection, so that older fossils will combine features possessed only in various parts by later, very different individuals.

> It is a common belief that the more ancient a form is, by so much the more it tends to connect by some of its characters groups now widely separated from each other. This remark no doubt must be restricted to those groups which have undergone much change in the course of geological ages; and it would be difficult to prove the truth of the proposition, for every now and then even a living animal, as the Lepidosiren, is discovered having affinities directed towards very distinct groups. Yet if we compare the older Reptiles and Batrachians, the older Fish, the older Cephalopods, and the eocene Mammals, with the more recent members of the same classes, we must admit that there is some truth in the remark. (Darwin 1859, 330–1)

Geographical distribution accounts for those birds of the Galapagos. How else does one explain them other than through evolution by natural selection? How, importantly, does one explain why they are so similar to birds on the mainland of South America? 'The most striking and important fact for us in regard to the inhabitants of islands, is their affinity to those of the nearest mainland, without being actually the same species' (Darwin 1859, 397). Speaking of the Galapagos Archipelago:

> The naturalist, looking at the inhabitants of these volcanic islands in the Pacific, distant several hundred miles from the continent, yet feels that he is standing on American land. Why should this be so? why should the species which are supposed to have been created in the Galapagos Archipelago, and nowhere else, bear so plain a stamp of affinity to those created in America? There is nothing in the conditions of life, in the geological nature of the islands, in their height or climate, or in the proportions in which the several classes are associated together, which resembles closely the conditions of the South American coast: in fact there is a considerable dissimilarity in all these respects. (Darwin 1859, 337–8)

Moving briskly on: systematics, morphology, embryology, this last named a special favourite of Darwin. Organisms that are very different as adults often had very similar embryos. Why? Because natural selection works only to separate adults. It is the same as in breeding. It is the adult forms and their differences that are prized, not the juvenile ones. Writing of puppies: 'I was told by breeders that they differed just as much as their parents, and this, judging by the eye, seemed almost to be the case; but on actually measuring the old dogs and their six-days old puppies, I found that the puppies had not nearly acquired their full amount of proportional difference' (Darwin 1859, 445). And so, finally, to the most famous passage in the history of science.

> It is interesting to contemplate an entangled bank, clothed with many plants of many kinds, with birds singing on the bushes, with various insects flitting about, and with worms crawling through the damp earth, and to reflect that these elaborately constructed forms, so different from each other, and dependent on each other in so complex a manner, have all been produced by laws acting around us. These laws, taken in the largest sense, being Growth with Reproduction; Inheritance which is almost implied by reproduction; Variability from the indirect and direct action of the external conditions of life, and from use and disuse; a Ratio of Increase so high as to lead to a Struggle for Life, and as a consequence to Natural Selection, entailing Divergence of Character and the Extinction of less-improved forms. Thus, from the war of nature, from famine and death, the most exalted object which we are capable of conceiving, namely, the production of the higher animals, directly follows. There is grandeur in this view of life, with its several powers, having been originally breathed into a few forms or into one; and that, whilst this planet has gone cycling on according to the fixed law of gravity, from so simple a beginning endless forms most beautiful and most wonderful have been, and are being, evolved. (Darwin 1859, 490–1)

Humans

One topic hardly mentioned in the *Origin* is the status of our species, *Homo sapiens*. This was not a function of doubt. Darwin never hesitated for one moment that we humans are part of the picture. His first private notebook speculations showing that he had grasped selection were on our species, and our thinking powers to boot.

> An habitual action must some way affect the brain in a manner which can be transmitted. – this is analogous to a blacksmith having children with strong arms. – The other principle of those children, which chance? produced with strong arms, outliving the weaker ones, may be applicable to the formation of instincts, independently of habits. – the limits of these two actions either on form or brain very hard to define. (Darwin 1987, N42)

But, other than a brief mention in the *Origin* to show that he was not ducking the issue – 'Psychology will be based on a new foundation, that of the necessary acquirement of each mental power and capacity by gradation. Light will be thrown on the origin of man and his history' (Darwin 1859, 488) – he stayed away from the topic. A wise decision because, at once, his theory was called the 'gorilla theory' or some such things and he was in danger of being immersed in what for him was somewhat of a side topic. However, twelve years later, in 1871, he did take up the challenge and, in *The Descent of Man, and Selection in Relation to Sex*, argued that our species, like all others, is a product of selection – mainly natural selection, but also that already mentioned, secondary mechanism, sexual selection, the struggle within a species by one sex for access to the other sex. As his subtitle tells us, there is a very extended discussion of this mode of selection, with much speculation – much very Victorian speculation – about its effects on humans.

> Man is more courageous, pugnacious, and energetic than woman, and has a more inventive genius. His brain is absolutely larger, but whether relatively to the larger size of his body, in comparison with that of woman, has not, I believe been fully ascertained. In woman the face is rounder; the jaws and the base of the skull smaller; the outlines of her body rounder, in parts more prominent; and her pelvis is broader than in man; but this latter character may perhaps be considered rather as a primary than a secondary sexual character. She comes to maturity at an earlier age than man. (Darwin 1871, vol. 2, 316–17)

Darwin was a great scientific revolutionary. With respect to his society, he was not always a great rebel.

Darwinian Revolution?

Move on now to the years after Darwin announced his theory of evolution through natural selection. There is a popular thesis that Darwin's contribution is much overrated. There were other evolutionists; Herbert Spencer, if anything, was more significant than Darwin. Moreover, although people certainly became evolutionists, few took up natural selection as the chief or even a significant cause. Historian Peter Bowler, author of *The Non-Darwinian Revolution: Reinterpreting a Historical Myth*, goes so far as to argue that it 'seems unreasonable for historians to claim that the turning point in the emergence of modern culture should be called a "Darwinian Revolution"' (Bowler 1988, 195). That's a pretty striking claim, so let's sort out the gold from the dross. We are talking now about science. Religion will come later. First, there is no doubt that a good number of leading, professional biologists, notably Thomas Henry Huxley, became evolutionists but were less than enthused by natural selection (Ruse 1996; Desmond 1998). A good part of the reason is that, if anything, for the kind of work they were doing, natural selection impeded their progress. As Darwin himself said – on the basis of nearly ten years of barnacle taxonomy – adaptation often conceals underlying similarities and homologies and it is the latter that give you guides to phylogeny, the route of evolutionary change. Morphologists and palaeontologists – Huxley was both – found natural selection a hindrance. Add to this, as Darwin himself admitted, natural selection demanded incoming variations – the building blocks of evolution – and while he was convinced that they are random in the sense of not occurring to need, while he was equally convinced that they are not random in the sense of being uncaused, he had little idea of the causes and consequent natures of the variations. One critic, the Scottish engineer Fleeming Jenkin, pointed out, using the kind of Victorian language that makes us uncomfortable these days, that if a white man found himself on an island of savages, notwithstanding his huge reproductive superiority, no one expected that in a generation or two the islanders would now be white. Jenkin shared with his fellow Victorians, including Charles Darwin, the assumption that whites were superior to non-whites, but the argument here is that the superior variations of the white man would be blended away. Darwin responded with a quasi-Lamarckian hypothesis ("pangenesis") about new variations always appearing, but truly no one was that convinced. The (allegedly) superior variations of the white man would be blended away. Darwin responded with a quasi-Lamarckian hypothesis ('pangenesis') about new variations always appearing, but truly no one was that convinced (Darwin 1868).

This all said, and admittedly it is much, particularly when you combine it with the fact that Herbert Spencer, who had a much more explicitly Lamarckian theory of change, was indeed getting much publicity, it is but part of the picture. For a start, in the strictly scientific world, selection (including natural selection) had supporters. Unsurprisingly, the agriculturalists, comfortable with artificial selection, responded favourably to natural selection. A leading textbook writer wrote about classification:

First the variations in form of this organ should be observed, including paleonto-logical evidence if possible; then its function or functions should be determined. With this knowledge endeavour to determine what was the primitive form of the organ and the various ways in which this primitive form has been modified, keeping in mind the relation of the changes in form of the organ to its functions. In other words, endeavour to read the action of natural selection upon the group of organisms as it is recorded in a single organ. The data thus obtained will aid in making a provisional classification of the group. (Comstock 1893, 41)

How much effect this had might be doubted. In the academic world, the aggies rate above only education. Below sociology even.

Something similar can be said about those who did use natural selection to understand fast-breeding organisms, the lepidopterists. Shortly after the *Origin* was published, Henry Walter Bates, a travelling companion in the Amazon of Wallace, came up with a brilliant explanation of the mimicry one finds in certain species of butterfly. He focussed on *Leptalis* butterflies, which mimic butterflies of the genus *Ithomia*. The latter are rejected by predating birds because the plants on which they feast are foul-tasting; the *Leptalis*, to the contrary, are quite tasty and historically were heavily predated, so natural selection has led them to take on the garb of the *Ithomia*. 'If a mimetic species varies, some of its varieties must be more and some less faithful imitations of the object mimicked. According, therefore, to the close-ness of its persecution by enemies, who seek the imitator, but avoid the imitated, will be its tendency to become an exact counterfeit, – the less perfect degrees of resemblance being, generation after generation, eliminated, and only the others left to propagate their kind' (Bates 1862, 511).

German biologist Fritz Müller, while living in South America, discovered other forms of mimicry. Closer to home, lepidopterists did sterling work on so-called industrial melanism, where butterflies and moths, heavily predated by birds, become darker and darker in response to trees getting ever sootier thanks to industrial pollution. 'I believe ... that Lancashire and Yorkshire melanism is the result of the combined action of the "smoke," etc., plus humidity [thus making the bark darker], and that the intensity of Yorkshire and Lancashire melanism pro-duced by humidity and smoke, is intensified by "natural selection" and "heredity tendency"' (Tutt 1891, 11). One enthusiast even wrote to Darwin about this.

My dear Sir,

The belief that I am about to relate something which may be of interest to you, must be my excuse for troubling you with a letter.

Perhaps among the whole of the British Lepidoptera, no species varies more, according to the locality in which it is found, than does that Geometer, Gnophos obscurata. They are almost black on the New Forest peat; grey on limestone; almost white on the chalk near Lewes; and brown on clay, and on the red soil of Herefordshire.

Do these variations point to the "survival of the fittest"? I think so. It was, therefore, with some surprise that I took specimens as dark as any of those in the New Forest on a chalk slope; and I have pondered for a solution. Can this be it?

It is a curious fact, in connexion with these dark specimens, that for the last quarter of a century the chalk slope, on which they occur, has been swept by volumes of black smoke from some lime- kilns situated at the bottom: the herbage, although growing luxuriantly, is blackened by it.

I am told, too, that the very light specimens are now much less common at Lewes than formerly, and that, for some few years, lime-kilns have been in use there.

These are the facts I desire to bring to your notice.

I am, Dear Sir, Yours very faithfully,

A. B. Farn

(Letter from Albert Brydges Farn, 18 November 1878 (Darwin 1985-, vol. 26, 440))

Unfortunately, as with agriculture, status decreed that none of this made major waves in the professional scientific community. Darwin got Bates a job as secretary to the Royal Geographical Society, which meant that he went from being an active naturalist to administrator of a club of well-heeled Victorians. Farn was a civil servant, and the same applied to many of the others. It was not that their science was bad – it was not – but rather that it did not have the kudos of new palaeontological discoveries from the American Midwest. Darwin was all too typical. One might have thought that with his family money he might have funded some selection experiments. He did not. Bates' work, introduced into later editions of the *Origin*, was tucked away towards the end rather than brought with a flourish into one of the earlier chapters. Farn seems to have gone unanswered. I suspect Darwin feared that selection experiments might prove negative, giving critics another weapon. Better to argue that selection works far too slowly to be observed and leave it at that.

Where natural selection was a big success was in Victorian culture, especially as represented by literature – fiction and poetry (Ruse 2017). In 1860, in Charles Dickens' weekly magazine *All the Year Round*, there were two very favourable articles on evolution, with special reference to natural selection. Opponents are referred to as 'timid'. Overall, this is a time for optimism.

> We are no longer to look at an organic being as a savage looks at a ship – as at
> something wholly beyond his comprehension; we are to regard every produc-
> tion of nature as one which has had a history; we are to contemplate every
> complex structure and instinct as the summing up of many contrivances, each
> useful to the possessor, nearly in the same way as when we look at any great
> mechanical invention as the summing up of the labour, the experience, the
> reason, and even the blunders, of numerous workmen. (Anon. 1860, 299)

Natural selection was a huge hit, and sexual selection even more so. This is the theme of George Eliot's *Daniel Deronda*, where the selfish anti-heroine Gwendolen Harleth marries Mallinger Grandcourt for his money alone. The selfless Daniel marries for love. At the end of the novel, Daniel sets off with his bride to the Promised Land, a new Moses aiming to build a home for his people. Gwen, however, has few prospects: 'It is because I was always wicked that I am miserable now' (Eliot [1876] 1967, 825).

Darwin enthusiast Edgar Rice Burroughs has Jane, at the end of *Tarzan of the Apes,* totally giving way to the demands of sexual selection. Fighting against 'the psychological appeal of the primeval man to the primeval woman in her nature', she obeys the stern dictates of Darwinian science. Nature decreed that she marry the apparent Lord Greystoke (William Cecil Clayton) instead of the (unacknowledged) true Lord Greystoke (Tarzan).

> Did not her best judgment point to this young English nobleman, whose love
> she knew to be of the sort a civilized woman should crave, as the logical mate
> for such as herself?
>   Could she love Clayton? She could see no reason why she could not. Jane
> was not coldly calculating by nature, but training, environment and heredity
> had all combined to teach her to reason even in matters of the heart.
> (Burroughs [1912] 1914, 340)

Fortunately, not all goes to plan. In the next novel in the series, Jane changes her mind and we're all set for twenty-five sequels.

The Twentieth Century

We move forward into the twentieth century. Well known is that a – many would say 'the' – major discovery was of the findings of Gregor Mendel, a monk in the Austro-Hungarian Empire, working around the same time as Darwin (Bowler 1989). Unlike Darwin and so many others, Mendel saw that the characters of heredity – what we today call genes – do not get blended down each generation but continue unchanged from generation to generation, unless altered spontaneously – that is, mutated. Rapidly, thanks to the work of Thomas Hunt Morgan and his associates, this new Mendelian genetics was given a physical basis, as units on the chromosomes in the nuclei of cells (Allen 1978). At the same time, the theory was extended to populations – the so-called Hardy–Weinberg law, destined to function, as does Newton's First Law of Motion ('Bodies continue in steady motion or at rest, unless acted upon by outside forces'), as an equilibrium law against which the effects of natural selection can be seen to play out. By 1930, the so-called population geneticists, notably Ronald Fisher in England and Sewall Wright in America, were formulating a Darwin–Mendel synthesis – natural selection at work in populations changing the ratios of Mendelian genes (Provine 1971). A point that will prove important later in this Element is that Fisher saw natural selection as doing all the heavy lifting; it has effects on populations as a whole, as they move from one gene ratio to another. Wright, to the contrary, saw populations splitting into small groups in which random effects are significant – genetic drift – and then, but only once this has produced new variations in the groups, these groups coming together and a kind of group-effect selection sorting through and declaring the winners. Natural selection has a role, for Wright, but it's nothing like the all-important role that it has in Fisher's version of the synthesis (see Figure 4).

Following the work of the population geneticists – a third was J. B. S. Haldane in England – the empiricists set to work to make a fully functioning theory. In Britain, under the name Neo-Darwinism, it was Oxford-based E. B. ('Henry') Ford and his school of ecological genetics who were important. In America, under the name Synthetic Theory, it was Russian-born fruit-fly specialist Theodosius Dobzhansky (1937) who was most influential, followed by German-born systematist Ernst Mayr (1942), palaeontologist George Gaylord Simpson (1944) and botanist G. Ledyard

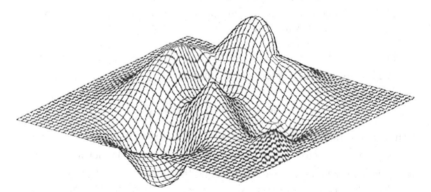

Figure 4 Sewall Wright's metaphor of an adaptive landscape
Note: Fisher thought that evolution involves whole populations (species) moving up or down under the force of natural selection. Wright saw species as broken into small populations at the tops of peaks. Normally a population on a lower peak cannot get to a higher peak because the valleys are non-adaptive. Genetic drift, a non-selective force, creates new (adaptive) features that make moving from lower to higher peaks possible.

Stebbins (1950). By 1959, the hundredth anniversary of the *Origin,* evolutionary biology had a complete paradigm. If we continue to use the language of Thomas Kuhn (1962), in the decades since Darwin we have seen a great deal of 'normal' science, extending and elaborating the now accepted foundations. This is true, although much of the work has been anything but normal. The coming of molecular biology was, at first, thought threatening. As it happened, much of the early influence was more that of handmaiden as it allowed evolutionists to ask and find answers to hitherto-unresolved questions, for instance about variations in populations. One area that has been developed in great detail and with much success is social behaviour, where new models have led to major new insights. And so it continues (Segerstråle 2000). Today there is much interest in molecular applications to problems of embryology – 'evo devo' (Arthur 2021). Many wonder if this is going to lead to a new paradigm, but others think that it, too, is part of normal, within-the-existent-paradigm science (Reiss and Ruse 2023).

One area that has seen great advance is that of human evolution (Harari 2015). To the amazement of virtually all, shortly after the declaration of a new paradigm, molecular techniques showed that the human line – hominins – had separated from the other great apes barely more than five million years ago. We left the jungles, became bipedal and, as has been said semi-facetiously, set out as hunter-gatherers on a five-million-year camping trip. In that time, our brains grew from ape size (about 400 cubic centimetres) to our present size (about 1,200 cc). We grew adept at making tools; through the development of language we became super-communicators; and we became the paradigm case of social animality, surpassing in respects even the hymenoptera (ants, bees and wasps). Obviously, today we are not always very social – First World War up to forty million dead, Second World War up to eighty million dead, Russian Civil War up to ten million dead and so the sad story continues. Whether this violence is genetic, cultural or a combination is much contested (Ruse 2022); we shall be taking it up later. For now, let us end our brief survey of evolutionary thinking and turn to religion.

2 Christianity

Faith

Revealed religion is the religion of faith – 'For I know that my Redeemer lives, and that at the last he will stand upon the earth' (Job 19:25). What is faith and why should we take it seriously? 'Now faith is the assurance of things hoped for, the conviction of things not seen' (Hebrews 11:1). I am not intending to be condescending when I say that faith is a bit like a Zoom conference call with God. Calvin spoke of a *sensus divinitatis.*

That there exists in the human minds and indeed by natural instinct, some sense of Deity, we hold to be beyond dispute, since God himself, to prevent any man from pretending ignorance, has endued all men with some idea of his Godhead, the memory of which he constantly renews and occasionally enlarges, that all to a man being aware that there is a God, and that he is their Maker, may be condemned by their own conscience when they neither worship him nor consecrate their lives to his service. (Calvin 1536, s. 3, 1)

The *sensus* is not faith itself but it leads to faith.

Faith, believers tell us, is more than just simple belief. To believe that 2+2=4 is not faith. Faith is in some sense a deep, overwhelming conviction that something is so. It is a bit like falling in love. I can think of no better example than when David Copperfield, in the novel of that name, meets his future first wife, Dora. He goes for the weekend to the house of the senior partner.

We went into the house, which was cheerfully lighted up, and into a hall where there were all sorts of hats, caps, great-coats, plaids, gloves, whips, and walking-sticks. 'Where is Miss Dora?' said Mr. Spenlow to the servant. 'Dora!' I thought. 'What a beautiful name!'

We turned into a room near at hand (I think it was the identical breakfast-room, made memorable by the brown East Indian sherry), and I heard a voice say, 'Mr. Copperfield, my daughter Dora, and my daughter Dora's confidential friend!' It was, no doubt, Mr. Spenlow's voice, but I didn't know it, and I didn't care whose it was. All was over in a moment. I had fulfilled my destiny. I was a captive and a slave. I loved Dora Spenlow to distraction!

She was more than human to me. She was a Fairy, a Sylph, I don't know what she was—anything that no one ever saw, and everything that everybody ever wanted. I was swallowed up in an abyss of love in an instant. There was no pausing on the brink; no looking down, or looking back; I was gone, headlong, before I had sense to say a word to her. (Dickens [1850] 1948, 390)

Faith is an overwhelming feeling of love, of significance, that is quite irresistible. Totally. John Hick, one of the most important philosophers of religion of the last century, wrote of his coming to faith.

An experience of this kind which I cannot forget, even though it happened forty-two years ago [1942], occurred – of all places – on the top deck of a bus in the middle of the city of Hull ... As everyone will be very conscious who can themselves remember such a moment, all descriptions are inadequate. But it was as though the skies opened up and light poured down and filled me with a sense of overflowing joy, in response to an immense transcendent goodness and love. (Hick 2005, 205)

You have no choice. Sometimes, you are not very keen on the idea. I suspect St Paul felt that way when, as Saul, he set out for Damascus to persecute Christians. C. S. Lewis, idol of earnest Protestants, felt this way.

You must picture me alone in that room in Magdalen, night after night, feeling, whenever my mind lifted even for a second from my work, the steady, unrelenting approach of Him whom I so earnestly desired not to meet. That which I greatly feared had at last come upon me. In the Trinity Term of 1929 I gave in, and admitted that God was God, and knelt and prayed: perhaps, that night, the most dejected and reluctant convert in all England. (Lewis 1955, 113)

I suspect I am not the only one made a little uncomfortable by the relish with which Lewis describes his futile resistance. Altogether too open to parody: 'In the Trinity Term of 1929 I gave in, and went to the brothel, the most dejected and reluctant fornicator in all England.' But the point is made. In fact, turning the tables on a cynic like me, that is the point. Faith is like an overwhelming sexual urge against which there can be no denial. Except it isn't really. I don't want to be a prude and say that going to a brothel is always a sign of weakness – I am sure I would have joined the queue in the First World War – but the person of faith experience would deny strenuously that faith is a sign of weakness. David falling for Dora is very human, but hardly very weak. It is true that she proves somewhat shallow, inadequate as a full partner for David, but he loves her dearly until the end. Having made the decision, weakness would have been turning on her.

Let's leave things here. Some people have faith. Others do not. Those who have faith say that it is an overwhelming emotion – notwithstanding that, for some (Mother Teresa), it flickers in and out at times – that gives insights into the ultimate questions of reality. I may not agree with such people, but I see no reason to assume at once that they are weak or inadequate or even self-deceiving.

The Bible

For Christians, for people of Christian faith, the Bible – the Old Testament, the story of the Jews, and the New Testament, the story of Jesus Christ – is definitive (McGrath 1997). It is the word of God, to be accepted on faith by Christians as completely true. Begin at the beginning with the account of Creation in the early chapters of Genesis (New Revised Standard Version).

[1] In the beginning when God created the heavens and the earth, [2] the earth was a formless void and darkness covered the face of the deep, while a wind from God swept over the face of the waters. [3] Then God said, "Let there be light"; and there was light. [4] And God saw that the light was good; and God separated the light from the darkness. [5] God called the light Day, and the darkness he called Night. And there was evening and there was morning, the first day. (Genesis 1:1–5)

Notice straight off the nature of this claim (Arnold and Beyer 2015). God, the Almighty, is a creator out of nothing. He is not just a designer, as is Plato's Demiurge in *Timaeus*. The Platonic god, whom Plato identifies with the form of the good, works on already-existing eternal substance, giving it order and purpose. We shall pick up on this when we get to natural theology. For the moment, let us continue with the Creation. Second and third days – land and sea and plants. Then the fourth day.

> [14] And God said, "Let there be lights in the dome of the sky to separate the day from the night; and let them be for signs and for seasons and for days and years, [15] and let them be lights in the dome of the sky to give light upon the earth." And it was so. [16] God made the two great lights—the greater light to rule the day and the lesser light to rule the night—and the stars. [17] God set them in the dome of the sky to give light upon the earth, [18] to rule over the day and over the night, and to separate the light from the darkness. And God saw that it was good. [19] And there was evening and there was morning, the fourth day. (Genesis 1:14–19)

Oh dear! We are already in trouble. We have light and dark on the first day, but it is not until the fourth day that we have the sun and the moon. The Bible is true, absolutely and completely. Then this. Augustine, the greatest – certainly the most influential – theologian of Christianity, wrestled with this one (Augustine [426] 1991, [413–26] 1998). Basically, his argument was that the ancient Jews were illiterate nomads and had God spoken to them in the civilized terms of fourth-century Romans, they would have had no idea of what He was talking about. So, He spoke to them not literally but allegorically. True, but in a form that these Jews could grasp. Thus, in the case of the clash between the creation of light and dark on the first day and the sun and the moon on the fourth day, we know that it cannot all be literally true because in our world we don't have light and dark without the sun and the moon. But it is treated 'as if', or glossed over, because the real message is that God could do what He wanted, and although something was going on, it is not really necessary to have the fine details:

> [I]ndeed, light was made by the word of God, and God, we read, separated it from the darkness, and called the light Day, and the darkness Night; but what kind of light that was, and by what periodic movement it made evening and morning, is beyond the reach of our senses; neither can we understand how it was, and yet must unhesitatingly believe it.
>
> For either it was some material light, whether proceeding from the upper parts of the world, far removed from our sight, or from the spot where the sun was afterwards kindled; or under the name of light the holy city was signified, composed of holy angels and blessed spirits, the city of which the apostle says, "Jerusalem which is above is our eternal mother in heaven"; and in another place, "For ye are all the children of the light, and the

children of the day; we are not of the night, nor of darkness." Yet in some respects we may appropriately speak of a morning and evening of this day also. For the knowledge of the creature is, in comparison of the knowledge of the Creator, but a twilight; and so it dawns and breaks into morning when the creature is drawn to the praise and love of the Creator; and night never falls when the Creator is not forsaken through love of the creature. (Augustine [413–26] 1998, Book XI, s. 7 – 'Of the Nature of the First Days, Which are Said to Have Had Morning and Evening, Before There Was a Sun')

Obviously, making a move like this opens the floodgates. Not, one hastens to say, necessarily in a bad way. The Bible is true, but not always literally true. Clearly, no one is going to say that the death on the Cross was not literal, that it is just an allegory, but a lot around it might be allegorical. Take the Resurrection. Some might insist on a literal reading. On that Sunday morning, Jesus literally did meet those women in the garden. Others might just as comfortably and sincerely read the whole story allegorically. The disciples on that Sunday, who had every reason to feel broken and without purpose, suddenly felt in their hearts that their leader, Jesus, really was alive and guiding them. So much so that they went out and preached, as with Peter, even unto death. True, but not literal.

The point is that biblical literalism is not 'traditional' Christianity, whatever that means (Numbers 2006; Larson 1997; Noll 2002). So those American evangelicals, literalists or fundamentalists, or (more recently) Creationists, are simply wrong when they claim to be the only true, traditional Christians. As historians have now shown us, they are idiosyncratic products of the early years of the Republic. Those were not easy times, particularly for those pushing back the frontiers or facing other challenges, notably the influx of immigrants from Europe, Ireland and the Continent, many of whom were Roman Catholics. The Bible, suddenly freely available thanks to mechanized forms of printing and book production, was a ready guide to the meaning of things and the rules for proper conduct, in the family and out in society: how a husband should treat a wife; how parents should treat children; how families should regard servants, including slaves; what obligations one has to the state and what one might expect in return; and much more that is involved in running daily life.

Not that the literalists have even been entirely true to their stated mission. They are into interpretation as much as any. Take, for instance, the heavy, and to outsiders somewhat odd, emphasis on the literal truth of the Deluge – as is shown by the huge influence of *Genesis Flood*. It is important not because of what it was back then but because it is seen as a harbinger of what is to come, namely end-times Armageddon when Jesus leads his forces in an epic battle against Satan and the forces of evil. Creationists are also quite happy to be allegorical when it suits them. The scarlet woman of the Apocalypse is rarely taken to be a real human being; it is the name for the Pope or the Roman Catholic Church as a whole, or – farther afield – Saladin or Islam as a whole. More recently, Saddam Hussein. Today, probably the Taliban.

Human Beings

Moving along through the week of Creation, we get fish and birds and land animals. And then, finally, on the sixth day, human beings.

> [26] Then God said, "Let us make humankind in our image, according to our likeness; and let them have dominion over the fish of the sea, and over the birds of the air, and over the cattle, and over all the wild animals of the earth, and over every creeping thing that creeps upon the earth."

> [27] So God created humankind in his image,
>   in the image of God he created them;
>   male and female he created them. (Genesis 1:26–7)

Take note. Right from the beginning humans are special. We are made in God's 'image' (Ruse 2021a). Understandably, gallons of ink have been spent on this one. Most would agree, however, that one important thing is that we are thinking, intelligent beings. We can reason things out. Most would also agree that a second important thing is that we are moral beings. We have a sense of right and wrong, and in some way we have the power to act on this. Free will. We would hardly be moral beings if we could never, ever do anything in the face of evil. Both of these attributes – intelligence, moral sense – play their role in the fact that we are superior to all other living things. We have 'dominion' over them. This does not mean that we own them or that we can simply do with them what we will. We are in charge of them, but that obviously includes responsibility (Rolston III 1999). Are men and women co-equals? Genesis 1 rather suggests so. As is well known, Genesis 2 has a different take on things. First come men: '[7] then the LORD God formed man from the dust of the ground, and breathed into his nostrils the breath of life; and the man became a living being.' Women come second and seem to exist to meet the needs of men. '[18] Then the LORD God said, 'It is not good that the man should be alone; I will make him a helper as his partner.' God remedied the omission.

> [21] So the Lord God caused a deep sleep to fall upon the man, and he slept; then he took one of his ribs and closed up its place with flesh. [22] And the rib that the Lord God had taken from the man he made into a woman and brought her to the man. [23] Then the man said,

"This at last is bone of my bones
and flesh of my flesh;   .
this one shall be called Woman,
for out of Man this one was taken."

24 Therefore a man leaves his father and his mother and clings to his wife, and
they become one flesh. (Genesis 2:21–4)

Heterosexual, apparently.

Now comes the big drama. We are made in the image of God. Hence, we are naturally good. God is good; so are we. But obviously we are not all that good. So how come we are sinners? Adam and Eve. These, apparently, were the first humans and they were put into paradise on Earth, the Garden of Eden. And trouble began.

1 Now the serpent was more crafty than any other wild animal that the Lord God had made. He said to the woman, "Did God say, 'You shall not eat from any tree in the garden'?" 2 The woman said to the serpent, "We may eat of the fruit of the trees in the garden; 3 but God said, 'You shall not eat of the fruit of the tree that is in the middle of the garden, nor shall you touch it, or you shall die.'" 4 But the serpent said to the woman, "You will not die; 5 for God knows that when you eat of it your eyes will be opened, and you will be like God, knowing good and evil." 6 So when the woman saw that the tree was good for food, and that it was a delight to the eyes, and that the tree was to be desired to make one wise, she took of its fruit and ate; and she also gave some to her husband, who was with her, and he ate. 7 Then the eyes of both were opened, and they knew that they were naked; and they sewed fig leaves together and made loincloths for themselves. (Genesis 3:1–7)

God was not pleased and kicked them out of the Garden of Eden, to work for a living and, in the case of women, to have babies rather painfully, not to mention to know their place:

I will greatly increase your pangs in childbearing;
    in pain you shall bring forth children,
yet your desire shall be for your husband,
    and he shall rule over you. (Genesis 3:16)

The main point is that because of the sin of Adam and Eve – mainly Adam because he is the male – all humans are contaminated. We are not born sinners, but we are born with a propensity to sin – which we do. 'Original sin.' And if proof is needed, Adam and Eve had two sons, Cain and Abel, and Cain promptly killed Abel. So, it goes down through the generations. There is barely an important person in the whole of the Old Testament who has never crossed the line. Indeed, it is some of the most favoured and most attractive who are the worst sinners. Above all, King David – so handsome, so brave, so talented. Yet, because of his lust for Bathsheba, he put her husband Uriah the Hittite in the centre of battle, where he was killed. David could (and did) now have her for his own.

This contamination by sin is not a satisfactory state of affairs. The Old Testament is not that big on individual survival after death. It is the continuance of the Israelites, taken as a whole, that counts. For individuals, it is a rather gloomy eternity in Sheol. 'For the living know that they will die, but the dead know nothing, and they have no more reward, for the memory of them is forgotten' (Ecclesiastes 9:5). 'The cords of Sheol entangled me; the snares of death confronted me' (Psalm 18:5). And more of this ilk. As time goes by, however, there evolves a more articulated and familiar afterlife, in major part because of outside influences, notably Greek. (*Phaedo*, Plato's dialogue about the day of Socrates' death, is very important.) By the time of the New Testament, heaven and hell were assumed as normal and expected. But how can sinners like us aspire to heaven, to blissful eternity with our Creator? It is here that Augustine showed his creative genius. Jesus, especially his death on the Cross, was a blood sacrifice to appease the Almighty and make us whole again. Substitutionary atonement. (There is some theological dispute as to whether we are made whole or declared whole.) The situation was so bad that it had to be God Himself who was the sacrifice. Mere mortals would not do.

One must add that not all Christians – especially those in the Orthodox tradition as well as some Western denominations (Quakers) – accept the Augustinian take on things. A serious alternative is the Incarnational perspective of (the Greek-born) Irenaeus of Lyons, a hundred years or more before Augustine. He saw the death on the Cross as an exemplar of perfect love. God sees humans as imperfect but on the way to improvement and redemption. Jesus comes among us and dies on the Cross, not as a blood sacrifice but as an exemplar of perfect love for us to emulate, on our way to salvation and unity with God. Jesus – God – is there beside us, helping us and urging us forward. One should also note that those in the Augustinian tradition have moved on from a rather crude blood-must-be-answered-with-blood sort of perspective, to be more in tune – as it seems to a non-believer, at least – with the Incarnational position of Jesus as an exemplar of perfect love. Of Aquinas, Dominican theologian Brian Davies writes:

> Aquinas is aware that Christians have used a range of words when reflecting on Jesus's saving work – words such as 'redemption', 'satisfaction', 'sacrifice', and 'atonement'. And he patiently tries to tease out the merits

and demerits of talking about Jesus using these terms. But his own account does not lay special emphasis on any of them. It also comes with the conviction that God can simply forgive sins by fiat. As Aquinas tries to develop his soteriology, therefore, he reflects on the *whole* of Jesus's life and teachings, including what seems to have been going on *as* he freely went to his death *following* opposition to him on the part of various Jews and Romans. (Davies and Ruse 2021, 210)

Fellow Dominican Herbert McCabe writes:

> If God will not forgive us until his son has been tortured to death for us then God is a lot less forgiving than even we are sometimes. If a society feels itself somehow compensated for its loss by the satisfaction of watching the sufferings of a criminal, then society is being vengeful in a pretty infantile way. And if God is satisfied and compensated for sin by the suffering of mankind in Christ, he must be even more infantile.
>
> (McCabe 1987, 92)

Moral Behaviour

Creation from nothing, humans superior, humans imperfect sinners, the hope of eternal life with our Lord after death. 'In my Father's house there are many dwelling places. If it were not so, would I have told you that I go to prepare a place for you?' (John 14:2). We have a sense of right and wrong and, through our intelligence, we are expected to act on this. Weak though we may be, we should do what is right and we should avoid what is wrong. But what exactly are right and wrong? Philosophers – and it is appropriate to turn to them here, even though we are not yet at natural philosophy and reason – distinguish between 'substantive ethics' – what should I do? – and 'metaethics' – why should I do what I should do? The Old Testament lays out substantive ethics in the Ten Commandments. The first ones are about religious observance – no god but God, no graven idols and so forth – before we get to the meat dealing with social behaviour.

[12] Honor your father and your mother, so that your days may be long in the land that the LORD your God is giving you.

[13] You shall not murder.

[14] You shall not commit adultery.

[15] You shall not steal.

[16] You shall not bear false witness against your neighbor.

[17] You shall not covet your neighbor's house; you shall not covet your neighbor's wife, or male or female slave, or ox, or donkey, or anything that belongs to your neighbor. (Exodus 20:12–17)

There are other rules and prohibitions throughout the Old Testament. For instance, in fighting, some things are allowed, while other things are prohibited. '[23] If any harm follows, then you shall give life for life, [24] eye for eye, tooth for tooth, hand for hand, foot for foot, [25] burn for burn, wound for wound, stripe for stripe' (Exodus 21:23–5). Some things are more specific. '[20] When a slaveowner strikes a male or female slave with a rod and the slave dies immediately, the owner shall be punished. [21] But if the slave survives a day or two, there is no punishment; for the slave is the owner's property' (Exodus 21:20–1). Women tend not to have full status and rights. When Sarah failed to conceive, she handed over Hagar, her servant, to Abraham. Then when Sarah did conceive, she got Abraham to kick Hagar out. Admittedly, Hagar was probably slave as well as woman, but still. There wasn't much equality later, either, especially when the Israelites got themselves kings. 'King Solomon loved many foreign women along with the daughter of Pharaoh: Moabite, Ammonite, Edomite, Sidonian, and Hittite women' (I Kings 11:1). Unsurprisingly: 'Among his wives were seven hundred princesses and three hundred concubines' (11:3). Homosexuals, too, were given less than full respect. 'You shall not lie with a male as with a woman; it is an abomination' (Leviticus 18:22). And then, in case anyone missed it: 'If a man lies with a male as with a woman, both of them have committed an abomination; they shall be put to death; their blood is upon them' (Leviticus 20:13).

The New Testament changes or amends some of these rules. Sometimes they are reinforced: '[27] You have heard that it was said, "You shall not commit adultery." [28] But I say to you that everyone who looks at a woman with lust has already committed adultery with her in his heart' (Matthew 5:27–8). Masturbators are in for a rough time: '[30] And if your right hand causes you to sin, cut it off and throw it away; it is better for you to lose one of your members than for your whole body to go into hell.' '[38] You have heard that it was said, "An eye for an eye and a tooth for a tooth." [39] But I say to you, Do not resist an evildoer.' '[43] You have heard that it was said, "You shall love your neighbor and hate your enemy." [44] But I say to you, Love your enemies and pray for those who persecute you.' Sometimes things sound depressingly familiar.

[11] Let a woman learn in silence with full submission. [12] I permit no woman to teach or to have authority over a man; she is to keep silent. [13] For Adam was formed first, then Eve; [14] and Adam was not deceived, but the woman was deceived and became a transgressor. [15] Yet she will be saved through childbearing, provided they continue in faith and love and holiness, with modesty. (1 Timothy 2:11–15)

⁹ Do you not know that wrongdoers will not inherit the kingdom of God? Do not be deceived! Fornicators, idolaters, adulterers, male prostitutes, sodomites, ¹⁰ thieves, the greedy, drunkards, revilers, robbers—none of these will inherit the kingdom of God. (I Corinthians 6:9–10)

⁵ Slaves, obey your earthly masters with fear and trembling, in singleness of heart, as you obey Christ; ⁶ not only while being watched, and in order to please them, but as slaves of Christ, doing the will of God from the heart. (Ephesians 6:5–6)

Finally, what of metaethics? The strong implication is that doing the right thing is doing what God wants you to do. To be honest, pinching an apple off a tree does not seem to be the very worst thing one might do. According to St Augustine, in the *Confessions*, apples have nothing on pears!

A pear tree there was near our vineyard, laden with fruit, tempting neither for colour nor taste. To shake and rob this, some lewd young fellows of us went, late one night (having according to our pestilent custom prolonged our sports in the streets till then), and took huge loads, not for our eating, but to fling to the very hogs, having only tasted them. And this, but to do what we liked only, because it was misliked.

(Augustine [396] 1998, s. 2.6)

Bad thing to do. 'It was foul, and I loved it; I loved to perish, I loved mine own fault, not that for which I was faulty, but my fault itself. Foul soul, falling from Thy firmament to utter destruction; not seeking aught through the shame, but the shame itself!' (Augustine [396] 1998, s. 2.6).

More seriously, of course, it is not the apple as such but the act of disobedience. And this disobedience seems to stem solely from what God wanted, not from external objective morality like that yielded by Plato's Theory of Forms. The Book of Job rather backs this up.

⁴ Where were you when I laid the foundation of the earth?
Tell me, if you have understanding.
⁵ Who determined its measurements—surely you know!
Or who stretched the line upon it?
⁶ On what were its bases sunk,
or who laid its cornerstone
⁷ when the morning stars sang together
and all the heavenly beings shouted for joy? (Job 38:4–7)

It is the story of the little red hen. I sowed it. I reaped it. I ground it. I baked it. I eat it. I made the world. My rules. Play by them.

The Proofs

Natural theology is to do with reason, most obviously whether God belief – Christian God belief – is a reasonable thing to have. Let us run quickly through the main arguments for God's existence, starting with the *ontological* argument. This is the argument that derives God's existence from His very definition. If you describe God as the All Perfect – and Christians would certainly want to do this – then He must have all the perfections. He must be all powerful, omnipotent. He must be all knowing, omniscient. He must be all loving. And so it goes. Does this God exist? This ontological argument, made first by Anselm of Canterbury (1077) in his *Proslogion* and restated by Descartes (1641) in his *Meditations*, is that existence is a perfection. It is better to exist than not to exist. Hence, since this is a perfection, God exists.

Experience suggests that people divide over the argument. Many – most? – think that it is just silly. Richard Dawkins in *The God Delusion* is just scathing; he cannot even bring himself to discuss it. There are, however, some who have a different attitude. While most would agree that it does not work – Kant pointed out perceptively that existence is not a predicate and so cannot be a perfection like being all powerful – it tells us something very important about the Christian God. He does not just exist, He exists necessarily. This point segues us into the next popular proof of God's existence, the causal or *cosmological* argument. Everything has a cause. The world is a thing. Therefore, the world has a cause. God. But, why then – to ask the Philosophy 101 question – does God not need a cause? Everything has a cause. God is a thing. Therefore, God must have a cause. The Christian response, the philosophers' response, is that God is not a thing like other things. They are contingent. They might not have existed. Adolf Hitler's mother might have had a miscarriage. God is not contingent. He exists necessarily. 2+2=4 does not have a cause, it did not come into being at some point, it will not go out of being at some point. It is necessary. Same with God. He is outside the causal chain. Someone who says, for instance, that the Big Bang does it all simply does not understand. That is part of the contingent world. God answers the question (called by Martin Heidegger the fundamental question of metaphysics): 'Why is there something rather than nothing?' Of course, not everyone agrees that the notion of necessary existence makes sense. Hume didn't. For now, I am just making the point that this is the claim for God, despite there being some debate about the nature of this existence. Anselm and Descartes rather imply that it is like logical existence: an object cannot be five pounds in weight and not five pounds in weight; the same goes for God. However, more general opinion – that of Aquinas – is that God has a kind of being of His own – 'aseity'. Not logical – that is for propositions – but still necessary.

The third of our arguments historically was, and undoubtedly still is, the most psychologically powerful of all the arguments for God's existence – and His nature. This is the argument from design or the *teleological* argument. Archdeacon Paley, at the beginning of the nineteenth century, gave the classic version:

> In crossing a heath, suppose I pitched my foot against a stone, and were asked how the stone came to be there; I might possibly answer, that, for any thing I knew to the contrary, it had lain there for ever: nor would it perhaps be very easy to show the absurdity of this answer. But suppose I had found a watch upon the ground, and it should be inquired how the watch hap-. pened to be in that place; I should hardly think of the answer which I had before given, that, for any thing I knew, the watch might have always been there. (Paley [1802] 1819, 1)

Why is this?

> For this reason, and for no other, viz. that, when we come to inspect the watch, we perceive (what we could not discover in the stone) that its several parts are framed and put together for a purpose, e. g. that they are so formed and adjusted as to produce motion, and that motion so regulated as to point out the hour of the day; that, if the different parts had been differently shaped from what they are, of a different size from what they are, or placed after any other manner, or in any other order, than that in which they are placed, either no motion at all would have been carried on in the machine, or none which would have answered the use that is now served by it. (Paley [1802] 1819, 1–2)

The argument is simple and straightforward. Organisms are akin to – indeed, they are – complex, functioning machines. This could not have happened by chance. Murphy's law rules supreme. If it can go wrong, it will go wrong. Something – something intelligent – must have made the watch. Something – something intelligent – must have made the eye and the hand and everything else we need to function. There is but one answer. A thinking being. God. No God, no nothing? 'Can this be maintained without absurdity? Yet this is atheism.'

In the eighteenth century, David Hume, in his *Dialogues Concerning Natural Religion*, hammered away at the argument. If you find something human-made that is complex and functioning, the chances are overwhelmingly probable that this is the work of more than one person, likely many people. Are we therefore to infer that there is not one god but many gods? If you find something human-made that is complex and functioning, the chances are overwhelmingly prob-able that this is the endpoint of many earlier, less-well-functioning prototypes.

Are we therefore to infer that there are or were many worlds inhabited by less successful organisms? In the end, Hume had to admit himself defeated. We have here an argument to the best explanation. As Sherlock Holmes said to Watson: 'How often have I said to you that when you have eliminated the impossible, whatever remains, *however improbable*, must be the truth?' (Conan Doyle [1890] 2003, 126)

> A purpose, an intention, a design, strikes every where the most careless, the most stupid thinker; and no man can be so hardened in absurd systems, as at all times to reject it. That Nature does nothing in vain, is a maxim established in all the schools, merely from the contemplation of the works of Nature, without any religious purpose; and, from a firm conviction of its truth, an anatomist, who had observed a new organ or canal, would never be satisfied till he had also discovered its use and intention. One great foundation of the Copernican system is the maxim, That Nature acts by the simplest methods, and chooses the most proper means to any end; and astronomers often, without thinking of it, lay this strong foundation of piety and religion. The same thing is observable in other parts of philosophy: And thus all the sciences almost lead us insensibly to acknowledge a first intelligent Author; and their authority is often so much the greater, as they do not directly profess that intention. (Hume [1779] 1963, 189–90)

Not only have we a proof of God's existence but, since the design is good, we know that the designer must be good. Just what the Christian needs.

One more argument – the argument from *miracles*. Do they not prove the existence of God? If you accept the Resurrection, that surely entails God belief. But is it not a little circular? Are you likely to accept the miraculous nature of the Resurrection without already believing in the existence of God? The same is true of other biblical miracles. Either you are going to be unconvinced unless you believe in God or – whether or not you believe in God – you are going to read passages allegorically and miracle free. Take Noah's Flood, supposedly miraculously brought on by God because He was mad at the way people were behaving. Without suggesting that others would read it this way, it has always struck me as having little or nothing to do with meteorology and a great deal to do with the futility of simplistic solutions. The clue is to be found after the Flood is over, in those events that are always omitted in primary school. Noah gets flaming drunk, his kid sees him stark naked in his tent, and laughs and goes and tells everyone. Sin is as much present after the Flood as before. What a lesson! What a lesson worthy of being included in the Bible. If only George W. Bush and Tony Blair had thought of it before they invaded Iraq.

More promising for God belief are non-biblical miracles. When I grew up in England in the 1940s, everyone thought that Dunkirk – when the British army escaped from the Germans by retreating across the Channel – was a miracle (Ruse 2001). For a start, for whatever inconceivable reason, Hitler halted his troops before they marched into Dunkirk and decimated the British. For a second, the Channel, usually so rough – think of the terrible storms upsetting the floating harbours after D Day – was like a millpond. All sorts of little ships could cross over and pick up soldiers. The British still think it a miracle and most would interpret miracle in this context as something brought on by God. Why? Because God made it possible for the British to regroup and continue the fight against Hitler. This last point is important. God did not do it all for us. He made it possible for us to do it all for us. That makes it authentic because that is the kind of God we worship. He has given us great talents. He expects us to use them. Remember the parable: The master gives one slave five talents.

> [19] After a long time the master of those slaves came and settled accounts with them. [20] Then the one who had received the five talents came forward, bringing five more talents, saying, 'Master, you handed over to me five talents; see, I have made five more talents.' [21] His master said to him, 'Well done, good and trustworthy slave; you have been trustworthy in a few things, I will put you in charge of many things; enter into the joy of your master.' (Matthew 25:19–21)

Dunkirk is the kind of miracle that leads to God belief. You might say that still you need first to be primed for God belief. That is probably true. But you are not simply calling Dunkirk a miracle because you believe in God. At the least, it is a feedback situation, where Dunkirk confirms your belief. You have independent evidence of the events of Dunkirk in a way that you do not have with the Resurrection.

Evil

Natural theology deals not only with the positive case for God but with the negative case against God: the problem of evil. Philosophers divide this into two: moral evil – Himmler – and natural evil – the Lisbon earthquake. How could we have either of these if God is all good and all powerful? The standard answers come readily. In the case of moral evil, it is all a question of free will. We are made in the image of God. What He does, He does freely. He did not have to create heaven and earth. He did not have to create human beings. It is to His credit that He did so, credit that would vanish were He simply a robot going through the motions. Same with us. Taking into account special cases – for instance when we are forced to do something – what we do, we do freely. In the middle of the Second World War, twenty-one-year-old Sophie Scholl of the White Rose group went to her death on the guillotine for having distributed pamphlets against the

Nazis. That is why she deserves great moral credit. She is a saint. She could have stayed silent. She did not. Henrich Himmler is the epitome of evil. He was the driving force behind the 'Final Solution', which in the end meant the death of six million Jews, mainly in such concentration camps as Auschwitz. It broke God's heart, but He saw that this was a consequence of human free will. There are great costs as well as great gifts to being made in His image.

Natural evil is usually explained as the consequences of things working blindly, mechanically. Gravity is a good thing, but that does mean that people will fall from ladders and get hurt or killed. If we say that God is all powerful, we do not mean that He can do the impossible. There are exceptions – Descartes was one – but generally it is not thought that God can make 2+2=5. It is no restriction on His being omnipotent, all powerful, that He cannot break the necessary truths of logic and mathematics. In recent years, so far impressed by this explanation of natural evil, there are some – unsurprisingly, those with a background in physics – who think that this points to an improved version of the teleological argument. Presumably, although He had to have some kind of gravity law, God could have made the law of gravity stronger or weaker than it is. There is no guarantee that the solar system would still work. Indeed, one very much expects that it would not. To such an extent is this world of ours so 'fine-tuned' that here we have another design argument for God. The 'anthropic principle' states that life could not exist if the laws were not such that life can exist, and the fact that such laws do exist cannot be mere chance. There must be a reason, or Reason, for this. God! God the physicist this time, rather than Paley's God the biologist.

Morality

Finally, what of morality? What does reason tell us about this? At the substantive level, much energy has been put into refining – if that is the right word – the rules found in the Bible. Most influential has been Aquinas' 'natural law theory'. Things that are natural are good. Things that are unnatural are bad. In the *Summa Theologica*, Aquinas writes:

> [G]ood has the nature of an end, and evil, the nature of a contrary, hence it is that all those things to which man has a natural inclination, are naturally apprehended by reason as being good, and consequently as objects of pursuit, and their contraries as evil, and objects of avoidance. Wherefore according to the order of natural inclinations, is the order of the precepts of the natural law.

Clarifying, he tells us:

> [I]n man there is first of all an inclination to good in accordance with the nature which he has in common with all substances: inasmuch as every substance seeks the preservation of its own being, according to

its nature: and by reason of this inclination, whatever is a means of preserving human life, and of warding off its obstacles, belongs to the natural law.

Next:

Secondly, there is in man an inclination to things that pertain to him more specially, according to that nature which he has in common with other animals: and in virtue of this inclination, those things are said to belong to the natural law, "which nature has taught to all animals," such as sexual intercourse, education of offspring and so forth.

Finally:

Thirdly, there is in man an inclination to good, according to the nature of his reason, which nature is proper to him: thus man has a natural inclination to know the truth about God, and to live in society: and in this respect, whatever pertains to this inclination belongs to the natural law; for instance, to shun ignorance, to avoid offending those among whom one has to live, and other such things regarding the above inclination.

(Aquinas [c.1269] 1981, IaIIae 94, 2)

Of course, Aquinas and other Christians would want to relate this to the moral precepts of the Bible. One can see that, in many respects, the two fit together well. Love and respect of parents. Avoidance of adultery. Not coveting or stealing the property of others. Note that, although Paul was a bit iffy about sexual relationships and, following him, Catholic priests are to remain celibate, overall sex between men and women is seen to be a good thing. Having children is natural. Also, though, one can see why homosexual relationships would be thought wrong. They are unnatural. Anuses are made for defecation, not for penetration by the penises of others.

Expectedly, in comparing the morality of reason and the morality of the Bible, there are tensions or felt need for elaboration. The Sermon on the Mount, for instance, can be read as a demand for pacifism, and it is so read by many Christians – the Mennonites and Quakers, for a start. However, equally, many do not want to be bound by such stern restrictions (Ruse 2018, 2022). For instance, at the beginning of the Second World War, most British very much did not want to go to war again, a mere twenty years after the dreadful First World War. But, equally, they felt a strong moral obligation to stop Hitler. Not to do so would be wrong. Looking back, as we realize the evils of the Third Reich, the killing of the Jews, for instance, most feel even more strongly that it would have been very wrong not to take up arms against the Nazis. Expectedly, Augustine had much to say on the matter. On the one side, it had to be shown that, Jesus notwithstanding, the Bible is far from entirely negative towards war and the military. No one was more beloved of God than David. Beloved, in part, because of his abilities and triumphs as a warrior. In the New Testament, when the centurion went to Jesus for help for his servant, Jesus did not turn on him and refuse to do anything on the grounds that he was a professional killer. He helped the servant. '[10] When Jesus heard him, he was amazed and said to those who followed him, "Truly I tell you, in no one in Israel have I found such faith"' (Matthew 8:10). On the other side, it had to be shown that there are standards of proper behaviour in war – a 'Just War Theory'. First, *jus ad bellum* – proper conduct in going to war. You must never provocatively start a war yourself. Fighting Hitler was right because he had invaded Poland and clearly was not going to stop there. 'Peace should be the object of your desire; war should be waged only as a necessity, and waged only that by it God may deliver men from the necessity and preserve them in peace. For peace is not served in order to the kindling of war, but war is waged in order that peace may be obtained' (*Letter to Boniface*, in Holmes 2005, 62–3). Then, *jus in bello* – proper conduct in war. Killing prisoners is wrong. 'Let necessity, therefore, and not your will, slay the enemy who fights against you. As violence is used against him who rebels and resists, so mercy is due to the vanquished or the captive, especially in the case in which future troubling of the peace is not to be feared' (Holmes 2005, 63).

What of the metaethical level? The answer falls straight out of the Thomistic position. Is not the will of God, as in Job, dreadfully arbitrary? If He had felt like it, could God have made the supreme moral principle that on Fridays we should push little old ladies in front of buses? Surely not. We are caught in the *Euthyphro* dilemma (so called because it first appears in Plato's dialogue of that name). Is the will of God in fact dictated by some outside objective set of rules? God does not have quite the dimension of freedom that one might assume. Or are the rules dictated by God, in which case we have the problem of the safety of little old ladies on Fridays? Aquinas' response is that morality is indeed the will of God, but God wills only the natural. Pushing little old ladies in front of buses is not natural: 'man has a natural inclination to know the truth about God, and to live in society'. You win both ways. God's choice, but God's choice is always what we would consider to be good. Of course, there is still a place for disagreement about what is natural. Is a woman preaching natural or unnatural? This is a question we shall encounter in the next chapter as we bring science and religion, evolutionary theory and Christianity into contact.

3 Confrontation

'Faith is an evil precisely because it requires no justification and brooks no argument' (Harris 2004, 3). In Sam Harris' *The End of Faith,* we learn that the truth is that religious faith is simply unjustified belief in matters of ultimate concern – specifically in propositions that promise some mechanism by which human life can be spared the ravages of time and death. Faith is what credulity becomes when it finally achieves escape velocity from the constraints of terrestrial discourse – constraints like reasonableness, internal coherence, civility, and candor. (Harris 2004, 3)

Chicago biologist Jerry Coyne agrees:

The danger to science is how faith warps the public understanding of science: by arguing, for instance, that science is based just as strongly on faith as is religion; by claiming that revelation or the guidance of ancient books is just as reliable a guide to the truth about our universe, as are the tools of science; by thinking that an adequate explanation can be based on what is personally appealing rather than what stands the test of empirical study. (Coyne 2015, 255–6)

Faith versus reason, science versus religion, evolution versus Christianity. Starting to unpack, let us return to our discussion of root metaphors. Darwinian evolutionary theory, we saw, is firmly located within or against the background of the machine metaphor, mechanism (Ruse 2021a, 2021b). The world is seen as a machine, unbroken law in action eternally, and Darwinism fits right in. Pause for a moment, however, and consider the implications of metaphor thinking, implications incidentally that Thomas Kuhn saw clearly when he introduced his notion of a paradigm, which he was to liken to metaphor (Kuhn 1993). A strength of metaphor is that it focusses attention. If we are thinking of the world as a machine, we are not going to ask questions about whether it is trying to lose weight. I speak of my beloved as a red, red rose; I am talking about her beauty and her freshness; perhaps, jokingly, I am teasing that she can be a little prickly; I am not talking about her mathematical abilities or whether she is a Catholic or a Protestant. These are meaningful questions, but not mine. Likewise with the world as a machine (Ruse 2010). First, I am not asking about where the materials came from or who put it together. I want a machine up and running. Second, I am not, as we have seen, talking about whether or not it is moral. Machines are machines are machines. Here we have a difference with the organic metaphor, where values are an inherent part of the picture. Third, with machines, I am not solving the body–mind problem. Leibniz in his *Monadology* made this point.

One is obliged to admit that perception and what depends upon it is inexplicable on mechanical principles, that is, by figures and motions. In imagining that there is a machine whose construction would enable it to think, to sense, and to have perception, one could conceive it enlarged while retaining the same proportions, so that one could enter into it, just like into a windmill. Supposing this, one should, when visiting within it, find only parts pushing one another, and never anything by which to explain a perception. Thus it is in

the simple substance, and not in the composite or in the machine, that one
must look for perception. (Leibniz 1714, 215)

Fourth, I am not talking about end times. Physicist Steve Weinberg (1977, 158)
famously said: 'the more the universe seems comprehensible, the more it also
seems pointless'. Why is this not a big surprise? Simply because the world as
a machine has no ultimate purpose. It might have such a purpose, but that is not
part of the metaphor. And this last point makes the general point, touched upon
in the last chapter when we said that Heidegger's (1959) fundamental question
of metaphysics – 'why is there something rather than nothing?' – cannot be
answered by reference to the Big Bang, that it is not that questions like 'why is
there something rather than nothing?', 'what is the justification of moral
understanding?', 'what is the relationship between body and mind?', 'what is
the point of it all?' are meaningless; rather, it is that these are not questions that
are part of science, that is, science under the machine metaphor – which
Darwinism is. Now, you might want to criticize faith for separate reasons.
Darwin and many others worry about different conflicting faith claims – Jesus
is the son of God (Christianity) or not (Judaism and Islam) – but that is
a different matter. As is the question of whether you think that the responses
of the religious – John Hick (1973) claimed that, despite differences, all were
pointing to a shared ineffable – are adequate. The point is that the scientist as
scientist, the evolutionist as evolutionist, the Darwinian as Darwinian, cannot
criticize the religious for saying that on faith the answer as to why there is
something rather than nothing is a Creator God. 'God created the heavens and
the earth.' You can disagree, but not on the grounds of being a Darwinian
because it is not saying something that Darwinism asserts or denies. Likewise:
'whoever breaks one of the least of these commandments, and teaches others to
do the same, will be called least in the kingdom of heaven; but whoever does
them and teaches them will be called great in the kingdom of heaven' (Matthew
5:19). Fair enough. But as a command, not part of evolutionary theory.
'So God created humankind in his image, in the image of God he created
them' (Genesis 1:27). Again, what all of this means with respect to the mind–
body problem is no concern of the Darwinian. And finally: 'In my Father's
house there are many dwelling places. If it were not so, would I have told you
that I go to prepare a place for you?' (John 14:2). Nice prospect, but nothing to
do with natural selection.

Biblical Truth

This is not to say that the religious never make claims on faith grounds about
areas properly within the realm of science, or to deny that the scientist has every

right to critique them. The Creationist, like Duane T. Gish, who says that the fossil record speaks against evolution and for Genesis is open prey. He is wrong, showing that there are clearly areas where religious claims – that is, claims made in the name of religion – and scientific claims clash. Here, it would be wrong to opt for faith over reason and evidence. These latter dictate that the Earth is not six thousand years old with all the creation having been done in six days. Creationists are wrong. Although, remember, most Christians are not Creationists and have little difficulty going along with the Darwinians on this point. (In fact, even at the time of the *Origin* most religious people – like Adam Sedgwick and William Whewell – admitted to a long lifespan for Planet Earth.) What, then, of more difficult questions? What of Adam and Eve and what of humans being special? Few evolutionists, certainly no Darwinians, are going to agree to a unique founding pair; nor, incidentally, are they going to be keen on accepting that sin entered the world only when that wretched apple was plucked and eaten. It is believed that the human population never dipped below about ten thousand – small, but more than two – and, in any generation, the parents were just as nice and nasty as their kids, and their children in turn are going to be just as nice and nasty as their parents – or their grandparents.

Expectedly, there are Christians – claiming not to be literalists but sounding very much like them – who have tried to wriggle out of this one. God chose two human beings uniquely to have the real power to decide between good and evil; in this respect, the others don't count. As is well known, in the 1980s claims were made (based on molecular evidence) that one female was the ancestor of all humans. Supposedly, 'Mitochondrial Eve' lived in Africa about 150,000 years ago. Of course, even if you accept this – and most scientists today would – it hardly makes Genesis all that plausible (Ayala 1995). No one is saying that she is the only human who was our ancestor. In my family's case, some chap named 'Ruse' who joined the British army in the late eighteenth century is the ancestor of all subsequent Ruses – in our line, at least. He was not the only ancestor shared by the Ruses, but he could be identified because, in our society, children take their father's last name. Moreover, he – like Mitochondrial Eve – was not the first sinner. That is, the first one in need of the death on the Cross. Suppose the first known Ruse killed his brother – shades of Cain and Abel. One presumes that the death of Jesus wiped the slate clean. But what about his dad who also killed his brother (the uncle of the first known Ruse)? We are that kind of family! Did the death on the Cross not apply to him or did he not need the death on the Cross or what? Truly, it seems better not to go down that route in the first place. This, of course, is quite separate from theological worries about blood sacrifices generally. In principle, they seem a lot more pagan than they are Christian. (Note, however, that in the last chapter I spoke to this problem and offered responses.)

Move on to the special status of humans. If one were working under the organic model, there would be no big problem. It is progressive. Acorn to oak. It is, moreover, progressive to human beings. Monad to man. Herbert Spencer writes: 'this law of organic progress is the law of all progress. Whether it be in the development of the Earth, in the development of Life upon its surface, in the development of Society, of Government, of Manufactures, of Commerce, of Language, Literature, Science, Art, this same evolution of the simple into the complex, through successive differentiations, holds through-out' (Spencer [1857] 1868, 245). Henri Bergson writes: 'not only does consciousness appear as the motive principle of evolution, but also, among conscious beings themselves, man comes to occupy a privileged place. Between him and the animals the difference is no longer one of degree, but of kind' (Bergson 1911, 34). And Edward O. Wilson writes: 'Human beings remain essentially vertebrate in their social structure. But they have carried it to a level of complexity so high as to constitute a distinct, fourth pinnacle of social evolution' (Wilson 1975, 380) (Figure 5).

Darwinism does not share this confidence. It is true that, starting with Darwin himself, there have been Darwinians who accept progress. 'Thus, from the war of nature, from famine and death, the most exalted object which we are capable of conceiving, namely, the production of the higher animals, directly follows' (Darwin 1859, 490). This, however, is more a function of his comfortable, upper-middle-class status in Victorian England than anything directly in his science. Earlier, he had seen far more clearly that the kind of theory he was formulating made no claims to inevitable progress. 'It is absurd to talk of one animal being higher than another. We consider those, when the cerebral structure / intellectual faculties most developed, as highest. A bee doubtless would when the instincts were' (Darwin 1987, B 74, which is taken from an earlier, 1837 notebook). 'Never use the words higher or lower', writes Darwin ([c.1847] 1990, 163, in the margin of his 1847, 6th ed. copy of Robert Chambers' 1844 work *Vestiges of the Natural History of Creation*).

> With respect to 'highness' and 'lowness', my ideas are only eclectic and not very clear. It appears to me that an unavoidable wish to compare all animals with men, as supreme, causes some confusion; and I think that nothing besides some such vague comparison is intended, or perhaps is even possible, when the question is whether two kingdoms such as the articulata or mollusca are the highest . . . . I do not think zoologists agree in any definite ideas on this subject; and my ideas are not clearer than those of my brethren.
>   (Letter to Joseph Hooker, 27 June 1854, DCP-LETT-1573)

The whole point of natural selection is that what wins is what wins. Sometimes it is better to be bigger, such as the giant birds like the moa that

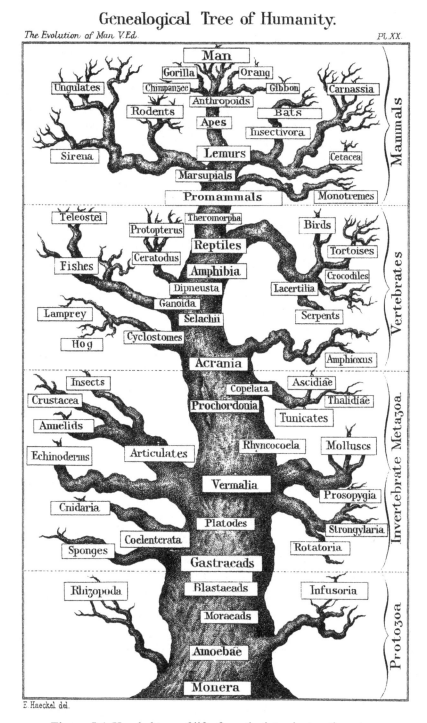

Figure 5 A Haeckel tree of life, from the late nineteenth century

Note: Humans are top in this drawing; however, Darwin's tree in the *Origin* makes no such claim. Darwin's aim is to show how groups split, not how they progress.

used to inhabit New Zealand. Sometimes it is better to be smaller, such as the hobbit *Homo floresiensis* on the island of Flores. Sometimes it is better to be intelligent; sometimes not. In the immortal words of palaeontologist Jack Sepkoski: 'I see intelligence as just one of a variety of adaptations among tetrapods for survival. Running fast in a herd while being as dumb as shit, I think, is a very good adaptation for survival' (Ruse 1996, 486). His teacher, Stephen Jay Gould, spoke of biological progress as 'a noxious, culturally embedded, untestable, nonoperational, intractable idea that must be replaced if we wish to understand the patterns of history' (Gould 1988, 319). In the case of humans, bringing up the asteroid that hit the Earth sixty-five million years ago, wiping out the dinosaurs and making for the success of the mammals who moved into the empty niches:

> Since dinosaurs were not moving toward markedly larger brains, and since such a prospect may lie outside the capabilities of reptilian design, we must assume that consciousness would not have evolved on our planet if a cosmic catastrophe had not claimed the dinosaurs as victims. In an entirely literal sense, we owe our existence, as large and reasoning mammals, to our lucky stars. (Gould 1988, 318)

Darwinism offers little support in favour of the Christian claim about our special status.

This said, if you think of the possibility of evolution elsewhere in the universe, perhaps somewhere, something human-like – humanoid – might have evolved. The restrictions need not be that stringent. The Christian story might have moved forward if we had six fingers and green skin. Gould (1985, 411) of all people agreed with this: 'I can present a good argument from "evolutionary theory" against the repetition of anything like a human body elsewhere; I cannot extend it to the general proposition that intelligence in some form might pervade the universe.' If you move out to the possibility of multi-verses, perhaps an infinite number of them, you could well have an embarrassment of riches. An infinite number of evolved human-like creatures. Alas, also with an infinite number of failures – would-be humanoids with the IQs of raw vegetables and the sporting ability of your average philosopher. One supposes that God, in His Wisdom, might have stood back and actualized only our evolutionary tree of life; but, I have a feeling that this might be cheating (Ruse 2021a). Perhaps this is a problem best left as an exercise for the reader.

Proofs

Move on now to the proofs for the existence of God. The ontological argument, remember, focusses on God's necessary existence. Richard Dawkins, also remember, was contemptuous. 'The very idea that grand conclusions could follow from such logomachist trickery offends me aesthetically, so I must take care to refrain from bandying words like "fool"' (Dawkins 2006, 81). Condescending also: 'I mean it as a compliment when I say you could almost define a philosopher as someone who won't take common sense for an answer' (83). Perhaps so – I guess I qualify because I don't accept as common sense that there should be something rather than nothing or that molecules can think. Going back to the discussion at the beginning of this chapter, having suggested that these questions about existence are outside the realm of empirical science, I see no reason to revise this judgement because Richard Dawkins' empirical science is evolution.

Much the same can be said about the cosmological argument. It works only if you think there can be a necessary being. The teleological argument, however, is rather different. Inasmuch as he accepted anything, Hume accepted the argument from design – that being does not have to have necessary being. Here, Darwinism really does have bite. The crux of the argument is that organisms seem as if designed – they demand understanding in terms of final causes. It is not good enough to say that the eye developed in such and such a way. We want to know why we have eyes in the first place. They exist in order that we can see. Plato argued that this points to a conscious designer – the Demiurge. Aristotle thought in terms of special forces or laws directing matter to desirable ends, ultimately somehow in unity with the Unmoved Mover. After Hume, Immanuel Kant worried about this problem. As a Newtonian, as a mechanist, these kinds of explanation are simply ruled out. And yet something is needed. In the end he came to the rather unsatisfactory conclusion that final-cause thinking is not real science but is in some way heuristic.

> The concept of a thing as in itself a natural end is therefore not a constitutive concept of the understanding or of reason, but it can still be a regulative concept for the reflecting power of judgment, for guiding research into objects of this kind and thinking over their highest ground in accordance with a remote analogy with our own causality in accordance with ends; not, of course, for the sake of knowledge of nature or of its original ground, but rather for the sake of the very same practical faculty of reason in us in analogy with which we consider the cause of that purposiveness. (Kant [1790] 1951, 36)

This did not stop Kant from being rather nasty about biology. The life sciences can never be brought up to the level of the physical sciences. '[W]e can boldly say that it would be absurd for humans even to make such an attempt or to hope that there may yet arise a Newton who could make comprehensible even the generation of a blade of grass according to natural laws that no intention has ordered; rather, we must absolutely deny this insight to human beings' (37).

This was the challenge that Darwin faced. What he did not do was deny final cause. In the *Origin* he addresses the problem of the cuckoo laying its eggs in the nests of other birds.

> It is now commonly admitted that the more immediate and *final cause* of the cuckoo's instinct is, that she lays her eggs, not daily, but at intervals of two or three days; so that, if she were to make her own nest and sit on her own eggs, those first laid would have to be left for some time unincubated, or there would be eggs and young birds of different ages in the same nest. If this were the case, the process of laying and hatching might be inconveniently long, more especially as she has to migrate at a very early period; and the first hatched young would probably have to be fed by the male alone.
>
> (Darwin 1859, 216–17, my italics)

The old cuckoo (the mother) lays eggs in the nests of other birds presumably because she has chance variations that cause her to do so. No good reason. However, it is these eggs that give rise to individuals that survive and reproduce better than others, so there is selection for this and, over time, we get birds doing it deliberately, as it were.

See what is happening? A (laying eggs in the nests of others) led to B (vigorous youngsters) led to A (more laying of eggs in the nests of others), until it was fixed by natural selection. (Kant to his credit saw that we have a kind of 'A leads to B leads to A' situation.) It is all done in terms of past (efficient) causes. But, because we see that A led to B in the past, we infer that an A in the present will lead to a B in the future. This is not ironclad. Final-cause explanations never are. I hammer the nail into the wood in order to build the house, but I don't get planning permission, so my efforts were in vain. I lay my eggs in the nests of others in order to produce more offspring, but a hurricane destroys the lot. I eat sweet things to get energy – a good move back in the Pleistocene – but now, having put on weight, I suffer a heart attack. Not such a good move today!

In other words, teleology without tears. Darwin shows us how we can get situations calling for final-cause explanation, without invoking a designer or whatever. Sherlock Holmes was right: the thing that Hume had thought impossible – design without intelligence – proves not to be impossible after all. Does this mean that the argument from design fails because of Darwin? It certainly no longer insists that you rely on God. To use Richard Dawkins' felicitous phrase, it makes it possible that you be an 'intellectually fulfilled atheist'. But, in itself, it does not insist that you be an atheist. You can still go on believing in God, even though, in itself, organic design – or 'design' – no longer compels you to believe in God. Perhaps not a death blow, but it does show that there is some bite to the confrontation of Darwinian evolutionary theory and Christian theology.

As we prepare to move on, honesty demands that not all Christian theologians and philosophers today take this kind of conclusion well. There is a feeling that critics fail to consider the way that chance in the universe is compatible with God's designing hand. Perhaps even a condition for that hand. Philosopher Michael Peterson writes:

> Paley-type arguments from design are based on a false dichotomy between chance and intelligent divine activity. Since natural selection produces adaptive fitness by sifting through random variations, direct divine designing activity would seem to be ruled out. When religious hopes are pinned on the rejection of chance, the mistaken presumption will always be that chance in the world as studied by science gives atheism a foothold. Science, of course, identifies various kinds of chance—from radioactive decay to the strike of an asteroid. But the claim that chance—conceived as nondetermined contingency— exists within the world is not inconsistent with standard theism. Furthermore, classical Christian ideas imply that contingency is essential in a relational universe in which creatures may freely choose to love God. What is inconsistent with theism and Christianity is the naturalist claim that chance is ultimate, that the natural world as a whole exists by chance and without divine purpose. Chance *within* a possible world must not be equated with chance *among* possible worlds.
>
> (Peterson and Ruse 2016, 111–12)

As I understand Peterson, the nature of the variations on which selection works is entirely chance. Where God shows His designing hand is in the flourishing or non-flourishing of organisms with the variations and the consequent design-like nature of the successful. I am not sure if this works. If the variations are produced by random quantum events then 'chance' might seem an appropriate term. But if the organisms are going to work in the end, the variations cannot be entirely chance. Variation A might beat variation B, and which variation an organism carries is entirely chance. But the situation cannot be so entirely chancy that only variation B appears. Perhaps that is where the multiple world possibility comes into play. In some world variation A must appear, otherwise talk of chance is empty. Whether this is enough is something that the reader must judge. I doubt Darwin would be convinced. At the end of the *Variation of Animals and Plants under Domestication*, in response to criticisms (akin to those of Peterson) from his American friend Asa Gray, he still worries that ultimately the presupposition is that chance is God-directed. Darwin writes:

> If an architect were to rear a noble and commodious edifice, without the use of cut stone, by selecting from the fragments at the base of a precipice wedge-formed stones for his arches, elongated stones for his lintels, and flat stones for his roof, we should admire his skill and regard him as the paramount

power. Now, the fragments of stone, though indispensable to the architect,
bear to the edifice built by him the same relation which the fluctuating
variations of each organic being bear to the varied and admirable structures
ultimately acquired by its modified descendants. (Darwin 1868, vol. 2, 430)

He continues:

> The shape of the fragments of stone at the base of our precipice may be called
> accidental, but this is not strictly correct; for the shape of each depends on
> a long sequence of events, all obeying natural laws; on the nature of the rock,
> on the lines of deposition or cleavage, on the form of the mountain which
> depends on its upheaval and subsequent denudation, and lastly on the storm or
> earthquake which threw down the fragments. But in regard to the use to which
> the fragments may be put, their shape may be strictly said to be accidental.
>
> (Darwin 1868, vol. 2, 431)

He then goes on to argue that we have an analogous situation in nature. The
variations are not random. They are caused by fixed laws, for which Gray/
Peterson give God credit. The point is that what happens to the variations is not
built into these laws. So, it is in this sense that the variations can be spoken of as
accidental. God has His Design, but from accidental variations. I don't think
Darwin thought this was enough. I don't think this is enough. Gray and Peterson
think it is enough. Let's leave things at that.

Move on to miracles. At one level, if you intend to believe in miracles then no
one is going to stop you, certainly not the evolutionist. If you think – if you
insist – that Jesus rose physically from the dead – that on the Saturday afternoon
he was already starting to get a bit smelly, and then on Sunday morning he was
up and chatting with his women visitors – then evolutionary theory is obviously
not going to stop you. You can say, truly, that science generally and evolutionary
theory in particular incline you to think that all events are natural, meaning
lawbound, and so miracles are less and less likely. That was Darwin's thinking
on the *Beagle*. But that does not mean that there are not miracles. It does, as
Darwin pointed out, tend to make you more critical of the purported evidence of
miracles. You end up more defending miracles than using them to prove God.
So be it. At another level, remember that not everyone would insist that
a miracle involves actual breaking of law. As I know, most English people,
then and now, were/are supremely indifferent as to whether the events at
Dunkirk meant that God intervened to change the weather or that the usual
laws were in action. A millpond Channel may be unlikely; it is not logically
impossible. It is rather all a matter of meaning. God made it possible for the
Brits to re-enter the fray and fight again. Included in the meaning here is that
God did not do it all for us; He made it possible for us to do it ourselves.
I suspect that many people would say that this does prove that there is a loving

God, a concerned Parent – perhaps more confidently than in relation to the Resurrection (certainly Noah's Flood) – because we know that it really did happen. No need for convoluted argument about how the Resurrection must be real because normally women would not be considered reliable witnesses. Whether evolution has a dog in this fight seems to me to be rather less obvious. It really isn't about evolution at all, for or against.

One thing you might worry about is whether, if you allow that miracles are all about meaning and no laws are actually broken, this allows for human free will. If God has determined it all beforehand, what choice did the British have? No credit at all to them, surely. Here making a point that will glide into our next topic, the problem of evil, it is important to note that theories of free will divide into two. There are the 'libertarians': these are not political activists like Ayn Rand; rather, they are philosophers who believe that human freedom stands outside law in some sense. This was the position of Kant. And there are 'compatibilists', notably David Hume but also others influenced by the Calvinist doctrine of predestination, such as equally notable Jonathan Edwards, who argue that you cannot have free will without things being lawbound! If I start taking my clothes off in the middle of campus, crying out, 'I am the returned Messiah', and there is no law, then I am crazy, not free. Freedom is working within law. If there are two students, one very clever and hardworking and the other not, I forecast correctly that the first student will get an A on the exam and the second an F. I am right. This does not abrogate the credit due to the first student or the discredit to the second. It was not chance. It was brought about because intellect affects performance as do training and effort. To go back to Dunkirk, if God set up all of the motions way back when – the Channel was going to be calm before Hitler's mum and dad met up – then we thank Him for making it all possible, although we still think that the Brits were free and fully deserving of all the credit we give to them.

There is one final item in dealing with miracles and Darwinism – and here the latter does rather prevent the former from being brandished as proof of a good God – and it is the problem of organic design, of final causes. Pre-Darwinians said that this demands an intervention by a designer – an out-of-the-natural-world intervention, otherwise known as a miracle. How else could we get the eye or the hand? In recent years this has been the central claim of a kind of reanimated Creationism – so-called Intelligent Design Theory (IDT). It is argued that organisms' design is so intricate – 'irreducible complexity' – that they could not have been put together gradually; unless all the parts were there from the first, they could not function. It is like having an automobile without wheels. Biologist Michael Behe writes:

> As an example from everyday life of an irreducibly complex system, I pointed to a mechanical mousetrap such as one finds in a hardware store. Typically, such traps have a number of parts: a spring, a wooden platform, a hammer, and other pieces. If one removes a piece from the trap, it can't catch mice. Without the spring, or the hammer, or any of the other pieces, one doesn't have a trap that works half as well as it used to, or a quarter as well; one has a broken mousetrap, which doesn't work at all. (Behe 1996, 353)

In the biological world, Behe chooses as an example the flagellum, a whiplike entity on certain bacteria that is used to propel them through the bodies that they invade. He argues that no part of the flagellum can be missing if it is to work. Hence, it had to be designed and put together in one fell swoop. And this calls for a miraculous intervention.

Expectedly, Darwinians say that no intervention is needed. The mousetrap has led to many happy hours, as evolutionists have shown that you can have a trap with four parts, with three parts, with two parts and even with one part. They are now working on a trap with no parts. All that is needed is that the trap, however awful, function better than competitors' traps. In the case of the flagellum, biologist Kenneth Miller writes: 'If we are able to find contained within the flagellum an example of a machine with fewer protein parts that serves a purpose distinct from motility, the claim of irreducible complexity is refuted.' He continues: 'the flagellum does indeed contain such a machine, a protein-secreting apparatus that carries out an important function even in species that lack the flagellum altogether. A scientific idea rises or falls on the weight of the evidence, and the evidence in the case of the bacterial flagellum is abundantly clear' (Miller 1999, 95).

The 'fine-tuning' argument encountered in the last chapter – the laws of physics demand certain constants, that there is no wiggle room on the nature of these constants, and hence, since we do in fact have them and everything works, it cannot be pure chance – likewise fails because of the empirical evidence. One of the favourite examples of supposed fine-tuning is the carbon atom. To get this atom we need three helium nuclei. Normally, this is not possible because the energy of carbon is way below that of three helium nuclei. However, it turns out that there is a radioactive form of carbon that has just the higher energy that is needed and so everything works out just fine. Yet, before you assume that you are on the way to God, Steven Weinberg (1999) points out that the three helium nuclei come together in a two-part process. First, two of them combine to make beryllium and then the third is added to make carbon. It turns out that here things need not be anything like so fine-tuned. The energy level that is crucial for the production of carbon is much more flexible. There is a range of possible energies that would do the job. In short, perhaps the laws we have were not quite so fine-tuned as this argument's enthusiasts suggest.

No irreducible complexity. No intelligent design. No fine-tuning. No miracles.

Evil

Two problems. Two solutions. First, divide the problem of evil into two parts: moral evil – Himmler – and natural evil – the Lisbon earthquake. The solution to moral evil: free will. The solution to natural evil: unfortunate effects of the working of blind law.

Just now, we started working on moral evil. At least, we started working on free will, most particularly the fact that we are the products of the lawbound process of evolution, understanding that, from the compatibilist perspective, natural selection as such is no barrier to free will.

> For what is meant by liberty, when applied to voluntary actions? We cannot surely mean that actions have so little connexion with motives, inclinations and circumstances, that one does not follow with a certain degree of uniformity from the other, and that one affords no inference by which we can conclude the existence of the other. For these are plain and acknowledged matters of fact. By liberty, then, we can only mean *a power of acting or not acting, according to the determinations of the will*; that is, if we choose to remain at rest, we may; if we choose to move, we also may. Now this hypothetical liberty is universally allowed to belong to every one who is not a prisoner and in chains. Here, then, is no subject of dispute. (Hume [1748] 2007, 68–9)

As it happens, Darwinism is not only compatible with free will but somewhat of an aid. When it comes to parental care, Darwinians distinguish two strategies (MacArthur and Wilson 1967): (1) there is r-selection when the environment fluctuates – have many offspring and let them care for themselves – as with ants; and (2) there is K-selection when the environment is stable – have just a few offspring but care for them – as with humans. It pours with rain: the queen ant is not bothered when a hundred foragers are washed away. It pours with rain: the mother human worries about her offspring. They went to McDonald's; will they return? Note what this means. Ants have little or no free will. If it starts to rain, they just keep going until they are drowned – or not. Humans must have free will. If it starts to rain, get out of it and under shelter. If it were sunny, you would stay outside, but it isn't, so you do something in response; you go to Starbucks for a latte until the storm is over. It is all entirely lawbound, but it involves a dimension of freedom not possessed by the ant. Dan Dennett (1984) draws attention to the Mars Rover. If it encounters an obstacle, it does not close down and do nothing. Nor does it wait to be controlled by humans back on Earth. It reacts itself and moves around and on its way, once again. 'The varieties of free

will worth having', to filch the subtitle of one of Dennett's books. The solution
to the problem of moral evil demands free will. Darwinism steps up to the plate.

Darwinism is equally helpful when it comes to natural evil. As it happens,
Darwin himself worried about this one.

> With respect to the theological view of the question; this is always painful to
> me.— I am bewildered.— I had no intention to write atheistically. But I own
> that I cannot see, as plainly as others do, & as I shd wish to do, evidence of
> design & beneficence on all sides of us. There seems to me too much misery in
> the world. I cannot persuade myself that a beneficent & omnipotent God would
> have designedly created the Ichneumonidæ with the express intention of their
> feeding within the living bodies of caterpillars, or that a cat should play with
> mice. Not believing this, I see no necessity in the belief that the eye was
> expressly designed. (Letter to Asa Gray, 22 May 1860, DCP-LETT-2814)

Richard Dawkins (1983) makes a useful suggestion. Simply put, if there is no
other way to get design effects – adaptations – other than through natural
selection – Lamarckism is false, saltations will not do – then God had no choice
but to let pain and suffering be part of the world picture. At least, He had no
choice if He wanted organisms, including humans. Creation had its costs, and
pain was the big one.

Darwin seems to have floated something like this. He continued his letter of
1860 to Gray:

> On the other hand I cannot anyhow be contented to view this wonderful
> universe & especially the nature of man, & to conclude that everything is the
> result of brute force. I am inclined to look at everything as resulting from
> designed laws, with the details, whether good or bad, left to the working out
> of what we may call chance.

Adding:

> Certainly I agree with you that my views are not at all necessarily atheistical.
> The lightning kills a man, whether a good one or bad one, owing to the
> excessively complex action of natural laws,—a child (who may turn out an
> idiot) is born by action of even more complex laws,—and I can see no reason,
> why a man, or other animal, may not have been aboriginally produced by
> other laws; & that all these laws may have been expressly designed by an
> omniscient Creator, who foresaw every future event & consequence.

(This is the voice of a deist. Later in the 1860s, Darwin became an agnostic.)

Morality: Organicism

Finally, what about morality? The traditional take on evolution and ethics is
generally known as Social Darwinism. Supposedly, at what philosophers call

the 'substantive level' – what should I do? – one sees in society as one sees in nature a brutal struggle for existence. There is certainly grist for the mill for this reading. Thus, Herbert Spencer writes:

> Blind to the fact that under the natural order of things, society is constantly excreting its unhealthy, imbecile, slow, vacillating, faithless members, these unthinking, though well-meaning, men advocate an interference which not only stops the purifying process but even increases the vitiation—absolutely encourages the multiplication of the reckless and incompetent by offering them an unfailing provision, and discourages the multiplication of the competent and provident by heightening the prospective difficulty of maintaining a family. (Spencer 1851, 323–4)

Thus, also, writes Scottish-born American robber baron Andrew Carnegie: 'The law of competition may be sometimes hard for the individual, [but] it is best for the race, because it insures the survival of the fittest in every department' (Carnegie 1889, 655). He is echoed by a leading sociologist: 'A drunkard in the gutter is just where he ought to be . . .. The law of survival of the fittest was not made by man, and it cannot be abrogated by man. We can only, by interfering with it, produce the survival of the unfittest' (Sumner 1884, 131). Nothing, however, compares to the claims by a former member of the German High Command, General Friedrich von Bernhardi. From his bestselling *Germany and the Next War*: 'War is a biological necessity'; hence: 'Those forms survive which are able to procure themselves the most favourable conditions of life, and to assert themselves in the universal economy of nature. The weaker succumb' (von Bernhardi 1912, 18).

One should say in defence of this school of thought, although it is hard to see any way of softening von Bernhardi – even after the war that Germany lost so badly, he was still at it – that most Social Darwinians showed a more creditable side. Spencer was far less concerned about making widows and children pay than about opening up society so that the poor but merited could work and succeed. Having stated that ethics is all about getting humans to the endpoint of evolution, he envisioned a kind of universal peace: 'there has followed the corollary that conduct gains ethical sanction in proportion as the activities, becoming less and less militant and more and more industrial, are such as do not necessitate mutual injury or hindrance, but consist with, and are furthered by, co-operation and mutual aid' (Spencer 1879, 21). Carnegie is famous for saying that no one should die rich. He put his philosophy into action by founding public libraries. Twentieth-century representatives of this mode of thinking, although they did their best to avoid being called Social Darwinians, thought in much the same way (O'Connell and Ruse 2021). Julian Huxley, biologist grandson of Thomas Henry Huxley (and older brother of novelist Aldous Huxley), campaigned for massive schemes for human betterment using the latest methods of technology. After the Second World War, he became secretary general of the United Nations Educational, Scientific and Cultural Organization (UNESCO). It was he who saw that Science was made part of the organization (Huxley 1948). Edward O. Wilson likewise campaigned for human betterment. His passion was environmental: 'a sense of genetic unity, kinship, and deep history are among the values that bond us to the living environment. They are survival mechanisms for us and our species. To conserve biological diversity is an investment in immortality' (Wilson 2002, 133).

How does one justify all this? What of foundations? Why should I do what I should do (which is what philosophers call metaethics)? Always, one sees that people are thinking within the organic model, for progress is the explicit foundation. We have seen Spencer's progressive philosophy. He ties this right in with his ethics. 'Ethics has for its subject-matter, that form which universal conduct assumes during the last stages of its evolution' (Spencer 1879, 21). Carnegie, as we have just seen – 'best for the race' – subscribes to the same philosophy. Von Bernhardi also: 'Without war, inferior or decaying races would easily choke the growth of healthy budding elements, and a universal decadence would follow.' And, in a nasty anticipation of *Mein Kampf*: 'Might gives the right to occupy or to conquer. Might is at once the supreme right, and the dispute as to what is right is decided by the arbitrament of war. War gives a biologically just decision, since its decision rests on the very nature of things' (von Bernhardi 1912, 10, quoted by Crook 1994, 83). More recently, thinkers in this mode are likewise eager progressionists. We have already seen Wilson on the topic. Julian Huxley was much influenced by Henri Bergson: 'When we look at evolution as a whole, we find, among the many directions which it has taken, one which is characterized by introducing the evolving world-stuff to progressively higher levels of organization and so to new possibilities of being, action, and experience' (Huxley 1943, 41–2).

Our conclusion thus far is that Social Darwinism is not – at the level of substantive ethics – necessarily anything like as bad as its reputation. Friedrich von Bernhardi is an exception. He really did try to live up to type. The irony is that he was supporting a position named after an Englishman when his whole being was directed at the downfall of the British! The Anglophones, however, from Spencer through to Wilson, were caught in an irony of their own. Metaethically they were/are not very Darwinian! Let us turn now, therefore, to a Darwinian approach – substantive ethics and metaethics.

Morality: Mechanism

Although no Social Darwinian, Thomas Henry Huxley agreed with the enthusiasts for this philosophy that the implications of Darwin's theory were bloody struggles for existence. Unlike them, he thought that our moral obligation is to resist such urges.

> Man, the animal, in fact, has worked his way to the headship of the sentient world, and has become the superb animal which he is, in virtue of his success in the struggle for existence. The conditions having been of a certain order, man's organization has adjusted itself to them better than that of his competitors in the cosmic strife. In the case of mankind, the self-assertion, the unscrupulous seizing upon all that can be grasped, the tenacious holding of all that can be kept, which constitute the essence of the struggle for existence, have answered. For his successful progress, throughout the savage state, man has been largely indebted to those qualities which he shares with the ape and the tiger; his exceptional physical organization; his cunning, his sociability, his curiosity, and his imitativeness; his ruthless and ferocious destructiveness when his anger is roused by opposition.
>
> But, in proportion as men have passed from anarchy to social organization, and in proportion as civilization has grown in worth, these deeply ingrained serviceable qualities have become defects. After the manner of successful persons, civilized man would gladly kick down the ladder by which he has climbed. He would be only too pleased to see "the ape and tiger die." (Huxley [1893] 2009, 51)

Despite his going down in history as Darwin's 'bulldog', Huxley rarely got Darwin right and he certainly did not do so here. In the *Descent*, Darwin made it very clear that he thought that selection (in humans) promoted co-operation and altruism.

> It must not be forgotten that although a high standard of morality gives but a slight or no advantage to each individual man and his children over the other men of the same tribe, yet that an advancement in the standard of morality and an increase in the number of well-endowed men will certainly give an immense advantage to one tribe over another. There can be no doubt that a tribe including many members who, from possessing in a high degree the spirit of patriotism, fidelity, obedience, courage, and sympathy, were always ready to give aid to each other and to sacrifice themselves for the common good, would be victorious over most other tribes; and this would be natural selection. (Darwin 1871, vol. 1, 166)

This is absolutely and completely the position of Darwinians today. We came out of the jungle and onto the plains about five million years ago. We became bipedal and our brains started to grow as we embarked on a life as hunter-gatherers, small bands (about fifty) living off prey that we caught and berries and the like that were there for the taking. We are not that fast – though we can keep going and exhaust our prey; we are not that strong – put Muhammed Ali against your local gorilla; we are, however, clever and sociable. We have the adaptations that enable our genes to make more copies of themselves. Out of evolutionary dirt grows the flower of human goodness (Greene 2013, 65).

Was there no downside? Clearly there was. Someone is pinching your wife; you are almost certain to react, possibly violently. Another band tries to move into your territory; you will probably kick up, although note that an equally good adaptive response may be to move away. If you start fighting, you might get hurt, although, as has been pointed out, almost always when fighting and the like occurs, it is done under the cloak of morality (Fiske and Rai 2014). It was wrong to pinch your wife; you have every right to get her back. Note that you are not just doing this for yourself, but to keep up the standards of the group. It is not going to work if everyone behaves like Canadian undergraduates in the early years of the pill. Virtuous violence! Yet, somehow, there seems to be a piece missing. If we are such very nice people then explain the horrendous figures given in Section 1 of deaths in the wars of the twentieth century. The explanation for this paradox is the advent of agriculture, about ten thousand years ago. Suddenly, there was need of a lot more children to work in the fields and on the farm. The result? A huge population explosion with much more competition for resources – and static resources that others might and would covet. A farmer could not just get up and walk away, thus war and the like began. 'The first clear evidence of warfare arrives with the development of agriculture' (Fry 2013, 112, quoting Raymond Kelly 2000, 2, in justification), 'following the "global conditions of warlessness that had persisted for several million years"'. The point is that war is not 'in the genes'. A popular picture of humans – in the tradition of Thomas Henry Huxley – is that we are 'killer apes', like those brutes at the beginning of the film *2001: A Space Odyssey.* This is quite misleading. Violence as we have it today is something brought on by culture. 'Our modern skulls house a stone age mind' (see Figure 6).

How does this mesh with the morality of the Bible? Obviously, overall, very well. Again and again the message is that we should help, be kind to, our fellow human beings. 'You shall love your neighbor as yourself' (Leviticus 19:18). 'In everything do to others as you would have them do to you; for this is the law and the prophets' (Matthew 7:12). 'You shall love your neighbor as yourself' (Mark 12:31). More specific exhortations fit in well, too. '[13] You shall not murder. [14] You shall not commit adultery. [15] You shall not steal. [16] You shall not bear false witness against your neighbor' (Exodus 20:13–16). This is not to say that everything will fit without some stretching. 'Blessed are the meek, for they will inherit the earth' (Matthew 5:5). My suspicion is that Darwinism can go but a small way with this. Vigour and a willingness to get stuck in and not be pushed around seem to me admirable traits in a hunter-gatherer.

Figure 6 Killer Ape, a US recruiting picture from the First World War (known then as the 'Great War')

What about the more extreme claims of Jesus? 'Do not resist an evildoer. But if anyone strikes you on the right cheek, turn the other also' (Matthew 5:39). 'You shall love your neighbor and hate your enemy. But I say to you, Love your enemies and pray for those who persecute you' (Matthew 5:44–5). Two comments. First, what Jesus demands is not quite so extreme if we go back to pre-agriculture days. There would be a premium on getting on in the group and a willingness to forgive and forget might well be a wise strategy. You don't have to be a softie, but, often, tolerance and generosity make a lot of sense. As far as enemies are concerned, presumably thinking now of other groups, again tolerance and the like will often make good sense. If fighting starts, someone is going to get hurt and it might be you. The best strategy might be to swallow your pride and walk away. There is no built-in genetic imperative insisting that you must always come to blows. Perhaps here one might argue that meekness is not such a bad thing after all. Meekness, that is, that stems from caution and common sense, not meekness that stems from coward-ice. Second, as we saw in the last chapter, ever since Jesus, Christians have been working hard to show that he did not really mean what he said he did! Take war, for instance. Darwinian biology meshes nicely with Just War Theory. Don't set out to fight. Be prepared, if need be, to defend your own or your allies. And if you do fight then do so in a restrained way. Darwinian biologists talk of 'reciprocal altruism', meaning if you scratch my back, I will scratch yours: 'as the reasoning powers and foresight of the members [of a tribe] became improved, each man would soon learn from experience that if he aided his fellow-men, he would commonly receive aid in return' (Darwin 1871, vol. 1, 163). Isn't this the reasoning behind *jus in bello*? 'Let necessity, therefore, and not your will, slay the enemy who fights against you. As violence is used against him who rebels and resists, so mercy is due to the vanquished or the captive, especially in the case in which future troubling of the peace is not to be feared' (Holmes 2005, 63).

Finally, let us take up some of the more contentious issues like the status of women. A lot of Christians today, and not just women, think that St Paul is about as non-Christian as one can be on this subject. (Fairness compels one to note that a lot of American evangelicals today think that Paul was spot on.) Darwinian theory has some interesting observations to make here. In hunter-gatherer days, women simply had to take on a full role. One suspects that there was a lot of infanticide for the good of the group. Virtuous violence. You simply could not afford to have half the tribe under twelve and half the adults spending most of their time caring for the under-twelves. Women had to pitch in. As the males were dashing around the prairies clad only in athletic supports and carrying spears, the women were back in camp making traps for catching smaller animals. No reason to think women naturally subservient or lacking in brain power. Then came agriculture and women turned into baby machines. Their second-class status followed. But it's not natural, if you mean 'in the genes'. As women are freed from being baby machines – household appliances like washers and driers and efficient contraception – women can start again to take equal place, as indeed they are doing. Ask any university teacher of fifty years' experience about the changing gender ratios in their classes. So, truly, Darwinism is on the side of those Christians who would give women equal roles, and against those who say that women should do what they are told and never, ever preach in church.

Metaethics and Realism

Let us turn now to the metaethical issues comparing Darwinism against Christianity. From what we have seen already, although Darwin can explain why we are moral beings and say much about the nature of this morality – substantive ethics – it cannot justify it. It is value neutral itself and sees the world itself as a machine and hence as value neutral. This means that if there is justification it must come from without, which – leaving God on the side for a moment – points to something like the Platonic Forms. 2+2=4 is an absolute, objective truth. Love your neighbour as yourself is an absolute objective truth. The trouble arises when you consider the non-directed nature of the Darwinian process. Darwin himself saw this. It is quite possible that we have a completely different morality.

> I do not wish to maintain that any strictly social animal, if its intellectual faculties were to become as active and as highly developed as in man, would acquire exactly the same moral sense as ours. In the same manner as various animals have some sense of beauty, though they admire widely different objects, so they might have a sense of right and wrong, though led by it to follow widely different lines of conduct. If, for instance, to take an extreme case, men were reared under precisely the same conditions as hive-bees, there can hardly be a doubt that our unmarried females would, like the worker-bees, think it a sacred duty to kill their brothers, and mothers would strive to kill their fertile daughters; and no one would think of interfering. Nevertheless the bee, or any other social animal, would in our supposed case gain, as it appears to me, some feeling of right and wrong, or a conscience. (Darwin 1871, vol. 1, 73)

I doubt we must become hymenoptera for something like this to obtain. Suppose we had what I call the 'John Foster Dulles' system of morality. Dulles was secretary of state under Eisenhower, during the Cold War in the 1950s. He hated the Russians. More than this, he thought that he had a moral responsibility to hate the Russians. However, he knew that they felt the same way about him. And so, everyone got on. Given its non-directed nature, it is at least conceivable that natural selection might have led us this way. In other words, against the background of an objective system of morality, we might go all the way through life thinking that we should hate people when truly we should love people. And if this isn't a *reductio ad absurdum* of objective morality then I do not know what is.

Two points. First, if there is no objective morality, why do we think there is? Obviously, because natural selection has led us this way. We 'objectify' our moral emotions. It is not just that I want to honour my mother and father; rather, I should honour my mother and father. Without objectification we are going to cheat, and morality goes out of the window. Second, isn't this the absolute barrier to reconciling Darwinism and Christianity? The first says that there is no objective morality; the Darwinian is a moral 'non-realist'. The second says that there is an objective morality; the Christian is a moral 'realist'. Note, however, what it means to be a Christian realist. It is not the case that such a person is committed to a separate Platonic world of values. Rather, it is all in the desire of God that we behave naturally. Loving our parents is natural. Hating our parents is unnatural. The Darwinian is likewise totally committed to morality being a matter of behaving naturally. We ought to love our children because it is natural. We ought not hate our children because it is unnatural. In the Nancy Mitford novel *The Pursuit of Love*, from the moment of birth, the anti-heroine Linda abandons her child Moira. One of the tensions of the novel – tension because, in many respects, we like and pity Linda – is how truly wrong this is. In short, Darwinian and Christian agree. Of course, the Christian puts this all in a God context, but this has nothing to do with the science. At the level of science, both are on the same side. There will be differences. The Roman Catholic refusing to let women be priests thinks that women are and always will be inferior. The Darwinian thinks that this is not necessarily the case. Obviously, in some sense science is involved here; in the end, though, it all comes down to the Catholic's religious belief, their faith in the God of the popes, and that is not science. No real clash here.

Epilogue

I said in my *Preface* that Darwinian theory is the offspring of Christianity. The case is made. First, Darwin's theory, like Christianity, is historical – a beginning and then forward through time. Not all religions are historical. Buddhism supposes no starting point. Not all theories of organisms are historical. Aristotle simply thought that all is eternal. Second, Darwin's theory, like Christianity, takes final cause very seriously. Organisms are not just thrown together; they show purpose – the eye for seeing, the hand for grasping. For the Christian, this was the work of a good God; for Darwin, of natural selection. This shared perspective is not accidental. Remember how Darwin started with Paley. Third, for Christianity there is a tree of life, located in the Garden of Eden. For Darwin, likewise, there is a tree. And then, fourth, there is the case of humans. For Christians, we are made in the image of God. Darwin wrestled with this one, feeling that there could be no inevitability. But, despite denials, he thought that he could get humans! This is from the third edition of the *Origin*:

> If we look at the differentiation and specialisation of the several organs of each being when adult (and this will include the advancement of the brain for intellectual purposes) as the best standard of highness of organisation, natural selection clearly leads towards highness; for all physiologists admit that the specialisation of organs, inasmuch as they perform in this state their functions better, is an advantage to each being; and hence the accumulation of variations tending towards specialisation is within the scope of natural selection. (Darwin 1861, 134)

Was this enough? Darwin certainly hoped so!

In the light of this relationship between Christianity and Darwin's theory, let us go back to Ian Barbour's fourfold division. It starts with (1) *conflict*. Science versus religion. Evolution versus Christianity. Obviously, certain interpretations of Christianity are going to conflict with evolution; you cannot be a six-day, six-thousand-year literalist and be an evolutionist of any kind. This said, we have seen that these literalists, fundamentalists or (more recently) Creationists are far from traditional Christians. St Augustine made it clear that one can and must often read the Bible allegorically. It is always true, but not necessarily always literally true. This said, my suspicion is that the conflicts between evolution and Christianity might be deeper than a lot of more liberal Christians allow. It is hard to see that a Darwinian can let pass the Augustinian theology of original sin – Jesus died on the Cross to atone for our sins because we are tainted by an inclination to sin that goes back to the fall of Adam and Eve in the Garden of Eden. For the Darwinian, for the organicist evolutionist also, there was no original pair, and whoever is picked out, their parents were sinners no less than they – in other words, it was not one unique act of disobedience that brought everything tumbling down. All of this is quite apart from the distaste one might have for blood sacrifices, although I will allow that that distaste is probably not something coming directly from Darwinian theory. (Actually, it might, if you take Darwinian views on morality seriously. I cannot imagine that substitutionary atonement was a big thing among hunter-gatherers.)

As we have seen, the Christian is not stuck with Augustine. There is the Incarnational option of Irenaeus. Here, it seems to me, there is little or no conflict – nor indeed with the more sophisticated Augustinians we have encountered. One can simply agree that humans are imperfect and that the death on the Cross was an exemplar of perfect love and not a sacrifice at all. What about other points of possible conflict? What about miracles? There seem various ways that the evolutionist can handle these. God simply intervened. End of argument. We take this on faith and do not look for or against empirical evidence. Or miracles, as interpreted, do not violate the laws of nature. Someone who interprets Dunkirk this way can be an enthusiastic Darwinian. If one goes with the Intelligent Design Theorists, then irreducible complexity does seem to call for miracles outside the course of nature. We have, however, seen reason not to take any of the claims of the IDT supporters too seriously. For a start, their science isn't very good. The same seems true of fine-tuning.

What then about faith itself? It is here that the New Atheists think we have a real clash between science and religion. Remember: 'Faith is what credulity becomes when it finally achieves escape velocity from the constraints of terrestrial discourse – constraints like reasonableness, internal coherence, civility, and candor' (Harris 2004, 3). Clearly, faith can lead to clashes with science. If one simply says that the Earth is only six thousand years old because one believes the Bible on faith, then one has a clash and science wins – at least it would if the people in power allowed a full and open debate. In America, there are always states seeking to evade the First Amendment separation of church and state. This said, Creationists always claim to have science on their side. *Evolution: The Fossils Say No!* does not sound like the work of a man who has given up on making scientific arguments. If one wants a classic example of Creationists at work, try *Genesis Flood*. 'Tremendous Erosion from Rainfall. Clouds Not the Source of the Deluge Rains. Enlarged Ocean Basins. Volcanic and Seismic Upheavals. Unprecedented Sedimentary Activity. Ideal Conditions for Fossil Formation. Uniformitarianism undermined by the Flood' (Whitcomb and Morris 1961, vii). And this is just the table of contents. Tedious detail after tedious detail. If someone were to claim that, surface appearances apart, faith is at work here convincing people of the truth of their positions, they would probably have a point. Gish needed something to explain his motivations for in his early years (at Berkeley) he had published in the *Proceedings of the National Academy of the Sciences* (Tsugita et al. 1960). How could he drop from the highest level of American science to what many would regard as its lowest level? Gish's switcheroos notwithstanding, it is simply that there is more than simple faith versus science. In any case, getting away from the literalists, when faith is invoked, it is for claims that were never and could not ever be scientific at all, a point to be re-emphasized as we turn to the next category.

And that is (2) *independence*. In his book with the punning title *Rocks of Ages,* Stephen Jay Gould introduced his notion of a Magisterium, a kind of world perspective not entirely unlike a paradigm. He argued that Magisteria cannot overlap – they are in a sense incommensurable – and that this applies to the science and religion relationship. Science is talking about things, while religion is talking about ethics, and so they are simply not in competition. Well, apart from the fact that it needs proving that things and ethics are incommensurable, it simply isn't the case that religion just talks about ethics. 'Why is there something rather than nothing?' isn't about ethics. Nor is the claim that there is a life hereafter.

This said, there is clearly something to be said for the independence view. Science and religion, evolution and Christianity are often simply not on the same board. 'Why is there something rather than nothing?' and 'Where are we going?' are simply not questions of science – for either mechanist or organicist – and so they are independent. What about morality, what it is and what its justification? The organicist thinks that his/her version of evolution can speak, not just to what it is but also to what justifies it – going up the chain and ever-increasing value. You can, but need not, put God behind this. Alfred North Whitehead ([1929] 1978), organicist through and through, would have put God behind it. Julian Huxley (1927) and Edward O. Wilson (2006), non-believers both, would not put God behind it. The Darwinian thinks you can, you must, agree that God does not have to be behind it. It just is. However, I see no reason why the Darwinian should not put God behind it. Darwinism and Christianity mesh, but this is no proof of God. It is surely proof that if you come to Christianity through faith or whatever then you have an independence position, but you can hold Darwinism and Christianity. At the end of the nineteenth century, conservative Anglican theologian Aubrey Moore wrote:

> The one absolutely impossible conception of God, in the present day, is that which represents him as an occasional visitor. Science has pushed the deist's God further and further away, and at the moment when it seemed as if he would be thrust out all together Darwinism appeared, and under the disguise of a foe, did the work of a friend. It has conferred upon philosophy and religion an inestimable benefit, by showing us that we must choose between two alternatives. Either God is everywhere present in nature, or he is nowhere. (Moore 1889, 73)

Different perspectives; independent perspectives. Commitment to one does not demand commitment to the other.

The mind–body problem is interesting. We are made in the image of God. Hence, we have mind and what that entails – intelligence and a moral sense. Nothing to stop a secular scientist agreeing; we have independence and different perspectives. However, note – independence or not – that nothing stops people, religious or secular, speculating in a philosophical manner about the mind–body problem. This would not exactly be an empirical exercise, but it would be one that, most comfortably, fits one's thinking on the mind–body problem with the empirical facts. The philosopher-mathematician William Kingdom Clifford, writing towards the end of the nineteenth century, speculated in this fashion:

> We cannot suppose that so enormous a jump from one creature to another should have occurred at any point in the process of evolution as the introduction of a fact entirely different and absolutely separate from the physical fact. It is impossible for anybody to point out the particular place in the line of descent where that event can be supposed to have taken place. The only thing that we can come to, if we accept the doctrine of evolution at all, is that even in the very lowest organism, even in the Amoeba which swims about in our own blood, there is something or other, inconceivably simple to us, which is of the same nature with our own consciousness, although not of the same complexity. (Clifford [1874] 1901, 38–9)

This position is known as 'panpsychic monism' – as suggested by Spinoza, mind and body are one substance, all-pervasive. Obviously, this does not solve much by way of empirical problems. It does not tell you why humans can think and presumably oysters cannot. It certainly does not prove whether God exists or not, unless you want to go the route of Spinoza and argue that God and nature – *Deus sive natura* – are one. Spinoza got kicked out of the synagogue for views like these. I am not sure the Vatican would be much more welcoming.

Next comes (3) *dialogue*. It might be said that already we have been dipping into this one. The discussion of panpsychism seems as much dialogue as anything else. This is hardly a worry; one expects the various categories to overlap some, though I cannot imagine the New Atheists having a dialogue with any Christian. Admittedly, Richard Dawkins once appeared on stage with the then Archbishop of Canterbury, Rowan Williams. Not much dialogue, however. As one commentator put it, 'it became a rather polite philosophical chess game, with the two opponents testing out each other's well-rehearsed defences'. One clear case where one seems to have genuine dialogue, or at least the opportunity for dialogue, is over the design argument. If we grant that, in the Age of Darwin, it no longer compels belief in a God, this does not mean that it is now without value. About his seminal philosophical work *A Grammar of Assent*, John Henry Newman wrote:

> I have not insisted on the argument from design, because I am writing for the nineteenth century, by which, as represented by its philosophers, design is not admitted as proved. And to tell the truth, though I should not wish to preach on the subject, for forty years I have been unable to see the logical force of the argument myself. I believe in design because I believe in God; not in a God because I see design. (Newman 1971, from a letter written in 1872)

He continued: 'Design teaches me power, skill and goodness – not sanctity, not mercy, not a future judgment, which three are of the essence of religion.' That surely sums it up for a lot of Christians. When they look at nature – the beauty of the wings of a butterfly, the majesty of a lion or a leopard, the language acquisition of a small child – they marvel and gives thanks and admiration to their Lord. As Newman says, that is not all that is to be said or felt about God, but it surely is a very important part. And if being made in the image of God means anything, it is surely using science to find out about how things evolved and how they work. 'I believe in design because I believe in God.'

Another area that seems promising for dialogue is that of morality. Both the Christian and the Darwinian see moral rules as centring on that which is natural. Both regard helping an old person to find their way as natural and good. Both regard cruelty to children as unnatural and bad. Neither is (necessarily) trying to convert the other. A Darwinian does not have to accept God to talk to a Christian. A Christian does not have to deny God to talk to a Darwinian. One presumes that this is true of Rowan Williams and Richard Dawkins. Perhaps rather less so of the Bishop of Oxford and Thomas Henry Huxley. One can nevertheless learn from the other and, in the end, what is dialogue but this? For instance, a secular Darwinian interested in the nature of war – and we have seen reasons why they could be, given what they now believe about the origins of war – might turn to Christian Just War Theory for insights about how war has been and could be fought. In fact, there is no 'might' about it. I, a secular Darwinian, have written two books on war: *The Problem of War: Darwinism, Christianity, and Their Battle to Understand Human Conflict* (Ruse 2018) and *Why We Hate: Understanding the Roots of Human Conflict* (Ruse 2022). In both, I discuss Just War Theory. Take, for instance, Desert Storm, during the first war (in 1991) against Iraq (when George H. W. Bush was president). It was explicitly fought on Just War Principles (O'Brien 1992). Darwinian and Christian can work together on studying Desert Storm – intentions, successes, failures. (A major reason why Just War Theory figured so prominently in Desert Storm was horrendous memories of the Vietnam War when, too often, the war was not waged on Just War Principles – think of Lieutenant Calley and the rape and slaughter of some five hundred people living in the village of My Lai.)

At a point like this, it is not just a question of congratulating each other on their moral insights. There are places where the Darwinian and the Christian might and do differ. Exploring the differences and the reasons can lead to new insights or reassessments of old insights. Take the status of women. Culturally, St Paul did not rate them as highly as men. One can see why, at least in some respects. It was thought natural that women be second-class citizens – second-class family members, for that matter. As Rousseau noted perceptively about Aristotle's endorsement of slavery, a major factor in these issues of social difference is the self-identification with their status of those below. Remember how many women spoke against votes for women, or who argued against the Equal Rights Amendment. In some respects, the Christian Church has moved on. There are female Episcopalian priests. Even bishops. Not with the Roman Catholics. There are no female priests, let alone a female cardinal. With the knowledge that Darwinians now have about reasons why women have been accorded lower status – we linked this in the last chapter with the coming of agriculture – and reasons why things are changing – machines to lighten domestic loads and safe and efficient contraception – one certainly sees opportunities for sharing and influencing. Who will come first, a female pope or a female president of the United States of America?

And so, finally, to (4) *integration*. Prospects for any kind of integration between Darwinism and Christianity seem slight. They may interact in a fruitful and harmonious way, but integration is another matter. The non-directedness of evolution and the denial of progress – biologically, humans are just another organism – seem to make genuine melding impossible. Things are otherwise for the organicist and it is no surprise to find that there have been celebrated attempts to fuse together evolutionary thinking and Christian doctrines. The best known is that of French palaeontologist and Jesuit Pierre Teilhard de Chardin. His *The Phenomenon of Man*, written in the 1930s although published only posthumously in 1955, owes as much to the evolutionary musings of Henri Bergson as it does to the theological musings of Jesus Christ. Teilhard (1955) sees the world as part of an overall process of evolution. It is a directed process, manifesting ever-greater complexity, from the inorganic to the organic, from the very simplest organisms up to the highest, the 'noosphere'. This is the home of humankind, culminating in something Teilhard called the 'Omega Point'.

> Our picture is of mankind labouring under the impulsion of an obscure instinct, so as to break out through its narrow point of emergence and submerge the earth; of thought becoming number so as to conquer all habitable space, taking precedence over all other forms of life; of mind, in other words, deploying and convoluting the layers of the noosphere. This effort at multiplication and organic expansion is, for him who can see, the summing up and final expression of human pre-history and history, from the earliest beginnings down to the present day. (Teilhard 1955, 190)

With his reading of the science backing him – Teilhard was perhaps the greatest French palaeontologist of the first half of the twentieth century – he identified the climax, the Omega Point, with God as incarnated in Jesus Christ.

> The universe fulfilling itself in a synthesis of centres in perfect conformity with the laws of union. God, the Centre of centres. In that final vision the Christian dogma culminates. And so exactly, so perfectly does this coincide

with the Omega Point that doubtless I should never have ventured to envisage the latter or formulate the hypothesis rationally if, in my consciousness as a believer, I had not found not only its speculative model but also its living reality. (Teilhard 1955, 293)

As a biologist, not a physicist, Teilhard wanted little to do with Heidegger's fundamental question 'Why is there something rather than nothing?'. Values, however, are central. 'With love, as with every other sort of energy, it is within the existing datum that the lines of force must at every instant come together' (Teilhard 1955, 190). He added: 'And, conquered by the sense of the earth and human sense, hatred and internecine struggles will have disappeared in the ever-warmer radiance of Omega. Some sort of unanimity will reign over the entire mass of the noosphere. The final convergence will take place in peace' (Teilhard 1955, 287).

Unsurprisingly, panpsychism is endorsed:

[W]e are logically forced to assume the existence in rudimentary form (in a microscopic, i.e. an infinitely diffuse, state) of some sort of psyche in every corpuscle, even in those (the mega-molecules and below) whose complexity is of such a low or modest order as to render it (the psyche) imperceptible— just as the physicist assumes and can calculate those changes of mass (utterly imperceptible to direct observation) occasioned by slow movement.

(Teilhard 1955, 301)

This is an integration far, far beyond anything envisioned by John Henry Newman. Unsurprisingly, Teilhard found few friends in the secular world. Nobel Prize winner Peter Medawar was brutal: '*The Phenomenon of Man* cannot be read without a feeling of suffocation, a gasping and flailing around for sense' (Medawar [1961] 1967, 99). Not that Teilhard's fellow Catholics were much better, writing of his publications: 'it is sufficiently clear that the above-mentioned works abound in such ambiguities and indeed even serious errors, as to offend Catholic doctrine' (O'Connell 2017, referring to the Monitum (Warning) by the Holy Office, 1962). It is not the place here to debate these judgements – Teilhard is being introduced as an example, not as the final truth – but it should be noted that not all of the reception was negative. Theodosius Dobzhansky, Russian Orthodox and much influenced by Sewall Wright, was president of the American Teilhard de Chardin Society. Julian Huxley, although an atheist, was much influenced by Bergson, so it is perhaps no surprise that he was president of the British Teilhard de Chardin Society. (Huxley wrote the *Preface* to the English translation of *The Phenomenon of Man*. One strongly suspects that it was Huxley who was Medawar's real target.)

With Teilhard and his friends and critics, we can bring this Epilogue – this whole Element – to an end. The relationship between evolutionary thinking – Darwinian evolutionary thinking in particular – and religion – Christianity in particular – is far more complex – and interesting – than dismissive thinkers, Creationists, New Atheists and fellow travellers allow. There is no one obviously right position. The hope is that enough material has now been presented for the reader to enter the fray and make judgements of his or her own.

References

Agassiz, E. C., ed. 1885. *Louis Agassiz: His Life and Correspondence*. Boston, MA: Houghton Mifflin.

Allen, G. E. 1978. *Thomas Hunt Morgan: The Man and His Science*. Princeton, NJ: Princeton University Press.

Anon. 1860. Species. *All the Year Round* 3 (58): 174–8.

Anselm of Canterbury [1077] 2008. *The Major Works*. Translated by B. Davies and G. R. Evans. Oxford: Oxford University Press.

Aquinas, St T. [c.1269] 1981. *Summa Theologica*. Translated by Fathers of the English Dominican Province. London: Christian Classics.

Arnold, B. T., and B. E. Beyer. 2015. *Encountering the Old Testament: A Christian Survey*. Grand Rapids, MI: Baker Academic.

Arthur, W. 2021. *Understanding Evo-devo*. Cambridge: Cambridge University Press.

Augustine. [426] 1991. *On Genesis*. Translated by R. J. Teske. Washington, DC: Catholic University of America Press.

[396] 1998. *Confessions*. Translated by H. Chadwick. Oxford: Oxford University Press.

[413–26] 1998. *The City of God against the Pagans*. Edited and translated by R. W. Dyson. Cambridge: Cambridge University Press.

Ayala, F. J. 1995. The myth of Eve: Molecular biology and human origins. *Science* 270: 1930–6.

Barbour, I. 1990. *Religion in an Age of Science*. New York: Harper and Row.

Bates, H. W. 1862. Contributions to an insect fauna of the Amazon Valley. *Transactions of the Linnean Society of London* 23: 495–515.

Behe, M. 1996. *Darwin's Black Box: The Biochemical Challenge to Evolution*. New York: Free Press.

Bergson, H. 1911. *Creative Evolution*. New York: Holt.

Bowler, P. 1988. *The Non-Darwinian Revolution: Reinterpreting a Historical Myth*. Baltimore, MD: Johns Hopkins University Press.

1989. *The Mendelian Revolution: The Emergence of Hereditarian Concepts in Modern Science and Society*. London: Athlone Press.

Boyle, R. [1686] 1996. *A Free Enquiry into the Vulgarly Received Notion of Nature*. Edited by E. B. Davis and M. Hunter. Cambridge: Cambridge University Press.

Browne, J. 1995. *Charles Darwin: Voyaging. Volume 1 of a Biography*. London: Jonathan Cape.

Burkhardt, R. W. 1977. *The Spirit of System: Lamarck and Evolutionary Biology.* Cambridge, MA: Harvard University Press.

Burroughs, E. R. [1912] 1914. *Tarzan of the Apes.* Chicago, IL: McClurg.

Calvin, J. 1536. *Institutes of the Christian Religion.* Grand Rapids, MI: Eerdmans.

Carnegie, A. 1889. The gospel of wealth. *North American Review* 148: 653–65.

Chambers, R. 1844. *Vestiges of the Natural History of Creation.* London: John Churchill.

    1846. *Vestiges of the Natural History of Creation*, 5th ed. London: John Churchill.

Clifford, W. K. [1874] 1901. Body and mind (from *Fortnightly Review*). In *Lectures and Essays of the Late William Kingdom Clifford.* Edited by L. Stephen and F. Pollock, 1–51. Vol. 2. London: Macmillan.

Comstock, J. H. 1893. Evolution and taxonomy. In *The Wilder Quarter Century Book*, 37–114. Ithaca, NY: Comstock Publishing.

Conan Doyle, A. [1890] 2003. The sign of the four. In *The Complete Sherlock Holmes*, Vol. 1, 97–184. New York: Barnes and Noble.

Cooper, J. M., ed. 1997. *Plato: Complete Works.* Indianapolis, IN: Hackett.

Coyne, J. A. 2015. *Faith versus Fact: Why Science and Religion Are Incompatible.* New York: Viking.

Crook, P. 1994. *Darwinism, War and History: The Debate over the Biology of War from the 'Origin of Species' to the First World War.* Cambridge: Cambridge University Press.

Darwin, C. [c.1845] 1990. *Charles Darwin's Marginalia*, Vol. 1. Edited by M. A. Di Gregorio with the assistance of N. W. Gill. New York: Garland.

    1859. *On the Origin of Species by Means of Natural Selection, or the Preservation of Favoured Races in the Struggle for Life.* London: John Murray.

    1861. *Origin of Species*, 3rd ed. London: John Murray.

    1868. *The Variation of Animals and Plants under Domestication.* London: John Murray.

    1871. *The Descent of Man, and Selection in Relation to Sex.* London: John Murray.

    1909. *The Foundations of the Origin of Species: Two Essays Written in 1842 and 1844.* Edited by F. Darwin. Cambridge: Cambridge University Press.

    1958. *The Autobiography of Charles Darwin, 1809–1882.* Edited by Nora Barlow. London: Collins.

    1985-. *The Correspondence of Charles Darwin.* Cambridge: Cambridge University Press.

1987. *Charles Darwin's Notebooks, 1836–1844*. Edited by P. H. Barrett, P. J. Gautrey, S. Herbert, D. Kohn and S. Smith. Ithaca, NY: Cornell University Press.

Darwin, E. [1794–6] 1801. *Zoonomia; or, The Laws of Organic Life*. 3rd ed. London: J. Johnson.

1803. *The Temple of Nature*. London: J. Johnson.

Davies, B., and M. Ruse. 2021. *Taking God Seriously: Two Different Voices*. Cambridge: Cambridge University Press.

Dawkins, R. 1983. Universal Darwinism. In *Evolution from Molecules to Men*, edited by D. S. Bendall, 403–25. Cambridge: Cambridge University Press.

2006. *The God Delusion*. New York: Houghton, Mifflin, Harcourt.

Dennett, D. C. 1984. *Elbow Room: The Varieties of Free Will Worth Wanting*. Cambridge, MA: MIT Press.

Descartes, R. [1641] 1964. Meditations. In *Philosophical Essays*, 59–143. Indianapolis, IN: Bobbs-Merrill.

Desmond, A. 1998. *Huxley: From Devil's Disciple to Evolution's High Priest*. London: Penguin.

Dickens, C. [1850] 1948. *David Copperfield*. Oxford: Oxford University Press.

Dijksterhuis, E. J. 1961. *The Mechanization of the World Picture*. Oxford: Oxford University Press.

Dobzhansky, T. 1937. *Genetics and the Origin of Species*. New York: Columbia University Press.

Draper, J. W. 1875. *History of the Conflict between Religion and Science*. New York: Appleton.

Eliot, G. [1876] 1967. *Daniel Deronda*. London: Penguin.

Fiske, A. P., and T. S. Rai. 2014. *Virtuous Violence: Hurting and Killing to Create, Sustain, End, and Honor Social Relationships*. Cambridge: Cambridge University Press.

Fry, D. P. 2013. War, peace, and human nature: The challenge of achieving scientific objectivity. In *War, Peace, and Human Nature: The Convergence of Evolutionary and Cultural Views*. Edited by D. P. Fry, 1–21. Oxford: Oxford University Press.

Gish, D. 1973. *Evolution: The Fossils Say No!* San Diego, CA: Creation-Life.

Gould, S. J. 1985. *The Flamingo's Smile: Reflections in Natural History*. New York: Norton.

1988. On replacing the idea of progress with an operational notion of directionality. In *Evolutionary Progress*. Edited by M. H. Nitecki, 319–38. Chicago, IL: University of Chicago Press.

1999. *Rocks of Ages: Science and Religion in the Fullness of Life*. New York: Ballantine.

Greene, J. 2013. *Moral Tribes: Emotion, Reason, and the Gap between Us and Them*. New York: Penguin.

Hall, A. R. 1983. *The Revolution in Science, 1500–1750*. London: Longman.

Harari, Y. N. 2015. *Sapiens: A Brief History of Humankind*. New York: Harper.

Harris, S. 2004. *The End of Faith: Religion, Terror, and the Future of Reason*. New York: Free Press.

Heidegger, M. 1959. *An Introduction to Metaphysics*. New Haven, CT: Yale University Press.

Herschel, J. F. W. 1830. *Preliminary Discourse on the Study of Natural Philosophy*. London: Longman, Rees, Orme, Brown, Green, and Longman.

Hick, J. 1973. *God and the Universe of Faiths: Essays in the Philosophy of Religion*. New York: St Martin's Press.

2005. *An Autobiography*. London: Oneworld Publications.

Hodge, C. 1874. *What Is Darwinism?* New York: Scribner's.

Holmes, A. F. 2005. *War and Christian Ethics*. Grand Rapids, MI: Baker.

Hume, D. [1748] 2007. *An Enquiry Concerning Human Understanding*. Oxford: Oxford University Press.

[1779] 1963. Dialogues concerning natural religion. In *Hume on Religion*, edited by R. Wollheim, 93–204. London: Fontana.

Huxley, J. S. 1927. *Religion Without Revelation*. London: Ernest Benn.

1943. *Evolutionary Ethics*. Oxford: Oxford University Press.

1948. *UNESCO: Its Purpose and Its Philosophy*. Washington, DC: Public Affairs Press.

Huxley, T. H. [1893] 2009. *Evolution and Ethics with a New Introduction*. Edited by M. Ruse. Princeton, NJ: Princeton University Press.

Jenkin, F. 1867. Review of 'The Origin of Species'. *North British Review* 46: 277–318.

Kant, I. [1790] 1951. *Critique of Judgement*. New York: Haffner.

Kelly, R. C. 2000. *Warless Societies and the Origin of War*. Ann Arbor: University of Michigan Press.

Kuhn, T. 1962. *The Structure of Scientific Revolutions*. Chicago, IL: University of Chicago Press.

1993. Metaphor in science. In *Metaphor and Thought*, 2nd ed. Edited by A. Ortony, 533–42. Cambridge: Cambridge University Press.

Larson, E. J. 1997. *Summer for the Gods: The Scopes Trial and America's Continuing Debate over Science and Religion*. New York: Basic Books.

Leibniz, G. F. W. 1714. *Monadology and Other Philosophical Essays*. New York: Bobbs-Merrill.

Lewis, C. S. 1955. *Surprised by Joy: The Shape of My Early Life*. London: Geoffrey Bles.

Lovejoy, A. O. 1936. *The Great Chain of Being*. Cambridge, MA: Harvard University Press.

Lucas, J. R. 1979. Wilberforce and Huxley: A legendary encounter. *Historical Journal* 22: 313–30.

MacArthur, R. H., and E. O. Wilson. 1967. *The Theory of Island Biogeography*. Princeton, NJ: Princeton University Press.

Malthus, T. R. [1826] 1914. *An Essay on the Principle of Population (Sixth Edition)*. London: Everyman.

Mayr, E. 1942. *Systematics and the Origin of Species*. New York: Columbia University Press.

McCabe, H. 1987. *God Matters*. London and New York: Continuum.

McGrath, A. E. 1997. *Christian Theology: An Introduction*, 2nd ed. Oxford: Blackwell.

Medawar, P. B. [1961] 1967. Review of *The Phenomenon of Man*. In *The Art of the Soluble*. Edited by P. Medawar. London: Methuen and Co.

Miller, K. 1999. *Finding Darwin's God*. New York: Harper and Row.

Mitford, N. 1945. *The Pursuit of Love*. London: Hamish Hamilton.

Moore, A. 1889. The Christian doctrine of God. In *Lux Mundi*. Edited by C. Gore, 57–109. London: John Murray.

Morris, H. M. 1999. Design is not enough! *Back to Genesis* 127: a–c.

Newman, J. H. 1971. *The Letters and Diaries of John Henry Newman, XXI*. Edited by C. S. Dessain and T. Gornall. Edinburgh: Thomas Nelson.

Noll, M. 2002. *America's God: From Jonathan Edwards to Abraham Lincoln*. New York: Oxford University Press.

Numbers, R. L. 2006. *The Creationists: From Scientific Creationism to Intelligent Design*. Standard ed. Cambridge, MA: Harvard University Press.

O'Brien, W. V. 1992. Desert Storm: A just war analysis. *St. John's Law Review* 66: 797–823.

O'Connell, G. 2017. Will Pope Francis remove the Vatican's 'warning' from Teilhard de Chardin's writings? *America* 21, November.

O'Connell, J., and M. Ruse 2021. *Social Darwinism (Cambridge Elements on the Philosophy of Biology)*. Cambridge: Cambridge University Press.

Paley, W. [1802] 1819. Natural theology. In *Collected Works*, Vol. IV. London: Rivington.

Peterson, M., and M. Ruse. 2016. *Science, Evolution, and Religion: A Debate about Atheism and Theism*. Oxford: Oxford University Press.

Provine, W. B. 1971. *The Origins of Theoretical Population Genetics*. Chicago, IL: University of Chicago Press.

Reiss, M., and M. Ruse. 2023. *The New Biology: The Battle between Mechanism and Organicism*. Cambridge, MA: Harvard University Press.

Rolston III, H. 1999. *Genes, Genesis and God: Values and Their Origins in Natural and Human History.* Cambridge: Cambridge University Press.

Ruse, M. 1975. Darwin's debt to philosophy: An examination of the influence of the philosophical ideas of John F. W. Herschel and William Whewell on the development of Charles Darwin's theory of evolution. *Studies in History and Philosophy of Science* 6: 159–81.

1996. *Monad to Man: The Concept of Progress in Evolutionary Biology.* Cambridge, MA: Harvard University Press.

2001. *Can a Darwinian Be a Christian?* Cambridge: Cambridge University Press.

2005. *The Evolution-Creation Struggle.* Cambridge, MA: Harvard University Press.

2010. *Science and Spirituality: Making Room for Faith in the Age of Science.* Cambridge: Cambridge University Press.

2017. *Darwinism as Religion: What Literature Tells Us About Evolution.* Oxford: Oxford University Press.

2018. *The Problem of War: Darwinism, Christianity, and Their Battle to Understand Human Conflict.* Cambridge: Cambridge University Press.

2021a. *A Philosopher Looks at Human Beings.* Cambridge: Cambridge University Press.

2021b. The Scientific Revolution. In *The Cambridge History of Atheism,* edited by S. Bullivant and M. Ruse, 258–77. Cambridge: Cambridge University Press.

2022. *Why We Hate: Understanding the Roots of Human Conflict.* Oxford: Oxford University Press.

Sebright, J. 1809. *The Art of Improving the Breeds of Domestic Animals in a Letter Addressed to the Right Hon. Sir Joseph Banks, K.B.* London: Privately published.

Secord, J. A. 2000. *Victorian Sensation: The Extraordinary Publication, Reception, and Secret Authorship of 'Vestiges of the Natural History of Creation.'* Chicago, IL: University of Chicago Press.

Sedley, D. 2008. *Creationism and Its Critics in Antiquity.* Berkeley: University of California Press.

Segerstråle, U. 2000. *Defenders of the Truth: The Battle for Science in the Sociobiology Debate and Beyond.* New York: Oxford University Press.

Simpson, G. G. 1944. *Tempo and Mode in Evolution.* New York: Columbia University Press.

Spencer, H. 1851. *Social Statics: Or, The Conditions Essential to Human Happiness Specified, and the First of Them Developed.* London: Chapman.

[1857] 1868. Progress: Its law and cause. *Westminster Review* LXVII: 244–67.

1879. *The Data of Ethics*. London: Williams and Norgate.

Stebbins, G. L. 1950. *Variation and Evolution in Plants*. New York: Columbia University Press.

Sumner, W. G. 1884. *What Social Classes Owe to Each Other*. New York: Harper and Brothers.

Teilhard de Chardin, P. 1955. *The Phenomenon of Man*. London: Collins.

Tsugita, A., D. T. Gish, J. Young, H. Fraenkel-Conrat, C. A. Knight and W. M. Stanley. 1960. The complete amino acid sequence of the protein of tobacco mosaic virus. *Proceedings of the National Academy of Science* 46: 1463–9.

Tutt, J. W. 1891. *Melanism and Melanochroism in British Lepidoptera*. London: Swan Sonnenschein.

Von Bernhardi, F. 1912. *Germany and the Next War*. London: Edward Arnold.

Wallace, A. R. 1858. On the tendency of varieties to depart indefinitely from the original type. *Journal of the Proceedings of the Linnean Society, Zoology* 3: 53–62.

Weinberg, S. 1977. *The First Three Minutes: A Modern View of the Origin of the Universe*. New York: Basic Books.

1999. A designer universe? *New York Review of Books* 46 (16): 46–8.

Whewell, W. 1840. *The Philosophy of the Inductive Sciences*. London: Parker.

Whitcomb, J. C., and H. M. Morris. 1961. *The Genesis Flood: The Biblical Record and Its Scientific Implications*. Philadelphia, PA: Presbyterian and Reformed Publishing Company.

White, A. D. 1896. *History of the Warfare of Science with Theology in Christendom*. New York: Appleton.

Whitehead, A. N. [1929] 1978. *Process and Reality: An Essay in Cosmology*. New York: Free Press.

Wilson, E. O. 1975. *Sociobiology: The New Synthesis*. Cambridge, MA: Harvard University Press.

2002. *The Future of Life*. New York: Vintage Books.

2006. *The Creation: A Meeting of Science and Religion*. New York: Norton.

Cambridge Elements ⁼

The Problems of God

Series Editor

Michael L. Peterson
Asbury Theological Seminary

Michael Peterson is Professor of Philosophy at Asbury Theological Seminary. He is the author of *God and Evil* (Routledge); *Monotheism, Suffering, and Evil* (Cambridge University Press); *With All Your Mind* (University of Notre Dame Press); *C. S. Lewis and the Christian Worldview* (Oxford University Press); *Evil and the Christian God* (Baker Book House); and *Philosophy of Education: Issues and Options* (Intervarsity Press). He is co-author of *Reason and Religious Belief* (Oxford University Press); *Science, Evolution, and Religion: A Debate about Atheism and Theism* (Oxford University Press); and *Biology, Religion, and Philosophy* (Cambridge University Press). He is editor of *The Problem of Evil: Selected Readings* (University of Notre Dame Press). He is co-editor of *Philosophy of Religion: Selected Readings* (Oxford University Press) and *Contemporary Debates in Philosophy of Religion* (Wiley-Blackwell). He served as General Editor of the Blackwell monograph series Exploring Philosophy of Religion and is founding Managing Editor of the journal *Faith and Philosophy*.

About the Series

This series explores problems related to God, such as the human quest for God or gods, contemplation of God, and critique and rejection of God. Concise, authoritative volumes in this series will reflect the methods of a variety of disciplines, including philosophy of religion, theology, religious studies, and sociology.

Cambridge Elements $\equiv$

The Problems of God

Elements in the Series

Divine Guidance: Moral Attraction in Action
Paul K. Moser

God, Salvation, and the Problem of Spacetime
Emily Qureshi-Hurst

Orthodoxy and Heresy
Steven Nemes

God and Political Theory
Tyler Dalton McNabb

Evolution and Christianity
Michael Ruse

A full series listing is available at: www.cambridge.org/EPOG